deer wild boar rabbit roe deer woodcock

Selous Rocher

The Perfect Life

of

HUNTERS

Manufrance

North America Morocco Spain Ireland

The Perfect Life

of

HUNTERS

deer wild boar rabbit roe deer woodcock

Selous Rocher

Manufrance

North America Morocco Spain Ireland

Text and Photographs

by

Éric Joly

BARRON'S

THE HUNTER'S MUSEUM

6

1

Introduction
page 8

Riding to Hounds
page 10

Guns
page 12

Engravings
page 16

GREAT NAMES IN HUNTING

18

2

Introduction
page 20

Life at Manufrance
page 22

Adolphe d'Houdetot: With Pen and Gun
page 24

Oberthur in the Land of the Animals
page 28

The Legendary Périnet Hunting Horn
page 32

Hunting Illustrated: A Source of Happiness
page 36

Selous: The Elephant Hunter
page 40

Doctor Rocher: I Must Have My Ducks!
page 42

Purdey: More than a Gun, a Legend
page 44

AROUND THE WORLD

46

Introduction
page 48

The Glory of the Somme
page 50

The Blind of the Big Shots
page 54

"Current Events" on the Saint Lawrence
page 56

The Brave Partridge of La Mancha
page 58

High-flying Pheasants in Search of Gentlemen
page 60

Hunters in Africa
page 62

Roissy: Rabbits Under the Jets
page 64

Chambord: The National Wild Boars
page 66

Rambling the Bogs of Ireland
page 70

Wood Pigeon Mountain
page 72

Turtledoves Under the Umbrella
page 76

The Quail of Taroudant
page 80

Falconry: A Hunt for the Nobility
page 82

GRAB YOUR GUNS!

84

Introduction
page 86

The Woodcock, Phantom of the Forest
page 88

Game from the Mountains
page 92

The Rabbit: A Game Animal That's Always Prized
page 96

Yearling Ducks: Summer Around the Ponds
page 100

Roe Deer, A Prolific Species
page 102

His Majesty the Deer: A Dream Trophy
page104

"Rocket" Partridge: Myth or Reality?
page 106

One Snow Goose Is Worth Two Canadas!
page 108

Searching for a Black Diamond
page 110

The Wolf: From Public Enemy to Noble Savage
page 112

The Beast of Gévaudan: A Mystery Never Resolved
page 116

THE HUNTER'S MUSEUM

THE HUNTER'S MUSEUM

Hunting becomes even more captivating when it's reflected in physical objects. For centuries, artists and artisans have found pleasure in embellishing the wilderness life of the woods runners. Some objects are plain and utilitarian, and others are true works of art.

"Hobbyists like to roam through sales rooms. . . ."

The great animal painters such as Oudry and Desportes in the eighteenth century, De Dreux, Reille, Reboussin, and John James Audubon a little later, have an undeniable following. The artists' talent takes root in the most varied places. Some collectors take a fancy to whistles, whips, hunting knives, game calls, decoys, powder flasks, game bags, hats, and many other things. All of these objects have a history. They have done service once before, in past lives. They have passed through the hands of numerous devotees, and this characteristic gives them an additional emotional value. Hobbyists like to roam through sales rooms, secondhand shops, and specialty shops in search of interesting and rare objects. Man! To find in some

obscure corner one of those famous coat racks inspired by Austria-Hungary that almost always show bears and cubs up to some amusing antics! To locate one of those exquisite Viennese bronzes that bring a partridge, a hare, or a wild boar back to life. To find in some attic an old, original mirror with a dove motif, one of the types made of aged wood and studded with little metal facets, not just flecks of glass. The devotee is interested in all kinds of things. Even a poorly stuffed animal placed into a decorative setting and covered with a glass globe can be appealing. How many hunters have decorated the interior of their house to reflect their passion? From the chandelier to the ashtrays and the floor lamps, the chairs, and the pictures on the wall—everything suggests excursions in the fresh air. Some pieces have only emotional value, but others may be true investments. That's surely the case with wooden duck decoys from Canada that have recently set record prices in sales rooms. When you follow your heart in making a purchase, you can make out quite well . . . .

From left to right:
Cartridge belts are no longer in fashion. On the other hand, the over-and-under shotgun is very popular and is replacing the side-by-side.

Beautiful wood and engraving are hallmarks of a great shotgun.

Harlequin duck decoy from Quebec: a thriving market in Europe as well as in the United States.

Side-lock guns are almost always associated with searching the English countryside for pheasants.

A sample of fine guns in a rack: a source of pleasure for every collector.

RIDING TO HOUNDS

Riding to hounds is a major part of the history of hunting. It was the preferred activity of kings and princes who owned their own packs of hounds. It also attracted painters and artists of all types who were inspired by the beauty of the dress, the grace of the large animals, and the baying of the pack.

The horn is used to communicate information to the members of the hunting party.

The hunting horn (right) is capable of producing some fairly elaborate and musical fanfares.

Trophy room at the Château de Cheverny. Displaying the antlers is part of the hunting ritual.

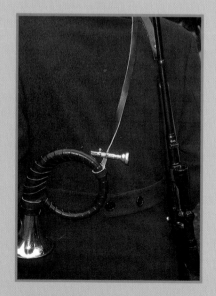

The German hunting horn, which makes a full circle, is also highly esteemed by hunters in other countries.

Closing in for the kill in the eighteenth century: the hunter carries a Dampierre-style horn.

Under the huntsman's whip: the pack gets ready to bound after the animal.

Blowing the horn. Horn blowers are classified according to their skill.

The rush for the spoils: the dogs pounce on the remains.

The attack: the dogs are unchained and take off in search of the quarry.

Breaking cover: the quarry has just emerged into the open. The object is to avoid losing it, for the quarry will use every trick it has.

GUNS

What an evolution has taken place from the first wheel lock guns to the modern firearms capable of firing thousands of rounds without a misfire! Hunting guns can also be real works of art, with inlays of mother-of-pearl, gold, silver filigree, and incomparable stock work.

Wheel lock harquebus from Thuringia, around 1650. A deer hunt is depicted on the fish-tail stock.
Museum of Hunting and Nature, Paris. Former collection of G. Pauilhac. Army Museum exhibit.

Harquebus with internal wheel from the beginning of the eighteenth century.
Arms Museum, Liege.

This fourteen-gauge double-barreled percussion shotgun with a carved walnut stock was made by Haaken-Plondeur in Liege in the nineteenth century.
Arms Museum, Liege.

1866 Winchester rifle.

Detail of the shotgun pictured above. The walnut fore end is carved with animal motifs.
Arms Museum, Liege.

View of the lock of a breech-loading wheel lock harquebus made in Bavaria in the sixteenth century.
Arms Museum, Liege.

Blued and damascened blunderbuss barrel.
Museum of Hunting and Nature, Paris.

1775 smoothbore with a fluted stock known as Mardid style.
Arms Museum, Liege.

This case contains a sixteen-gauge double-barreled percussion shotgun made in Liege in 1829 for the Prince of Orange.
Arms Museum, Liege.

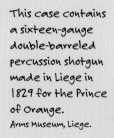

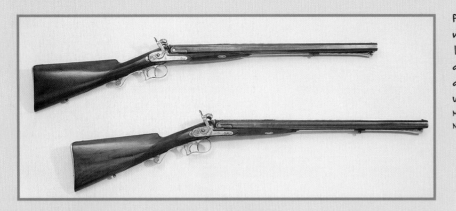

Pair of big-game rifles made by Devisme in 1835. The hammers and all the hardware are of steel engraved with animals.
Museum of Hunting and Nature, Paris.

The lockplate on this shotgun created by Anton and Ferdinand Lebeda in Prague in 1857 depicts trophies and a camp.
Arms Museum, Liege.

Wild boar tusks add a good decorative effect to the gun cabinet.

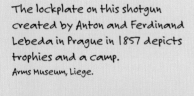

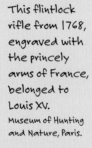

This flintlock rifle from 1768, engraved with the princely arms of France, belonged to Louis XV.
Museum of Hunting and Nature, Paris.

Presented at the Universal Exposition of Paris in 1900, this Purdey and Sons twelve gauge is a true masterpiece of gun making from the beginning of the century.
Arms Museum, Liege.

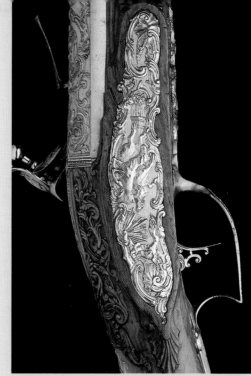

The quality of the engraving adds significant value to a firearm. The motifs are arabesques and representations of game animals.

Side-lock guns. This action assures reliability and allows very fine tuning.

This flintlock smoothbore with a chased lock escutcheon plate in the rocaille style that was fashionable in Europe in the eighteenth century once belonged to Frederick the First of Sweden.
Arms Museum, Liege.

Over-and-under shotgun manufactured by Browning (twentieth century).
Arms Museum, Liege.

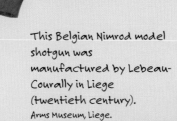

This Belgian Nimrod model shotgun was manufactured by Lebeau-Courally in Liege (twentieth century).
Arms Museum, Liege.

ENGRAVINGS

Prints, lithographs, engravings: hunting is present everywhere. Hunting with hounds has captured the attention of artists ever since the Middle Ages. Only in the nineteenth century did artists become interested in small-game hunting with firearms.

Illumination from the *Treatise on Hunting* by Gaston Phoebus, count of Foix. The treatise dates from fifteenth-century France.

Woodcock in full flight by French hunter and illustrator Joseph Oberthur (twentieth century).

Plate from the *Hunter's Almanac* from the end of the eighteenth century depicting wolf tracks.

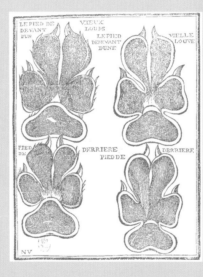

Hunting wild boar. Woodcut taken from a hunting manual from the sixteenth century.

Chamois hunting in the Bavarian Alps. Nineteenth-century engraving.

La chaſſe du Cerf.

Je suis le Cerf, a cauſe de ma teſte
Par les Grecz ſus Ceratum ſurnommé,
Car en beauté i'excede toute beſte,
Dont a bon droict ilz m'ont ainſi nommé.
Pour le plaiſir des Rois ie ſuis donné,
De iour en iour les Veneurs me pourchaſſent
Par les Foreſtz: Je ſuis abandonné
A tous les Chiens, qui ſans ceſſe me chaſſent.
Si du docte Phebus auez commancement
De Venerie, icy traduicte groſſement:
Je me ſuis voulu mettre en toute diligence
Vus en pouuoir donner parfaicte intelligence.
L 3   De

Illustration for a work on hunting by Jacques du Fouilloux (sixteenth-century France).

Woodcut of a hare, from a sixteenth-century hunting manual.

Pieces from a parlor game (end of nineteenth century).

Duck hunting in Canada at the end of the nineteenth century.

Woodcock hunting. Engraving published in Hunting Illustrated (nineteenth century).

Deer hunting; miniature from the fifteenth century.

Facsimile of a print from the book Treatise on Hunting by Gaston Phoebus (fifteenth century).

GREAT NAMES IN HUNTING

GREAT NAMES IN HUNTING

Hunting has its heroes and great hunters. Some have even been immortalized in current language. The French speak of a *tartarinade*, a feat of bragging that would have done justice to Tartarin, a mediocre hunter but a very accomplished liar. Diana, goddess of the hunt, is eternal, and Saint Hubert, patron saint of hunters, is commemorated on the calendar.

"He would travel the world over to bag a new trophy."

Bishop Hubert really existed, but his conception of hunting is not very reliable. Too bad! Count Zaroff was a hunter of men, and that has left its mark on the history of cinema. Later on, the big guns known as the sabers became enshrined in the hunting memory. These men had a habit of firing thousands of rounds every year and shooting game with mechanical regularity. They included Count Clary, Quelen, and lots of other powder addicts. Lord Malmesbury, a grouse specialist, one day went through about 1,500 rounds in bagging 1,070 birds, connecting with 72 percent of his shots. For centuries, the person who could shoot down the maximum amount of game was considered a great hunter. He

would travel the world over to bag a new trophy. He could be found in India, Africa, America, and China. Theodore Roosevelt and Paul Niedeck are good examples. The houses of these celebrities are real museums, with walls studded with trophies from all parts of the world. Fame can also come to a corporation. That's the case with Manuf and its fantastic cave of Ali Baba, and with the Périnet company and its wonderful hunting horns. However, the evolution of ideas and the emergence of ecological thinking brought about a change of course. A new breed of hunters arose toward the end of the nineteenth century. They were as much naturalists as they were shooters. An example is the good doctor Oberthur with his hundreds of plates depicting wild game; Count Lippens who ended up putting his gun away so he could better serve the swamp birds of Belgium; Doctor Rocher, who knew all there was to know about ducks; and Francois Sommer, who created a foundation for nature conservancy. These celebrities are also distinguished for their writing. Tony Burnand captivated hunters in the last century. His ability as a storyteller has been passed on for successive generations to enjoy.

From left to right:
Engraving from the beginning of the century: this young hunter will earn a couple of pennies for his duck.

Opening day of the hunting season in 1912. Scene from a village festival.

Wild goat hunter in the Pyrenees at the start of the twentieth century.

A hare as "big as a mule," a trophy esteemed by French hunters.

A string of woodcock in Brittany. The bag limit is now set at three birds per day per hunter.

A trilogy still sought after by fans of Manufrance.

These pictures clearly show the vital importance that an industrial site has for a region.

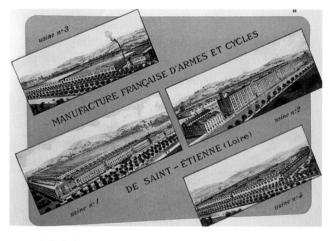

A bewildering catalog where you could find anything from the smallest bolt to an elephant gun, including bicycles and low-cut shoes.

Life at Manufrance

A symbol of life in the great outdoors, Manuf remains graven in the hearts of French hunters, who have religiously saved catalogs from the great age.

It was an erudite book, always at arm's reach in the library. This magic book had the astonishing ability to renew itself year after year. People waited for it. They coveted the new edition. They spent hours turning its pages. Ali Baba's cave! Hundreds of hunting and fishing items were described in minute detail: from a tiny sparrow decoy to big-game rifles capable of dispatching a buffalo or an elephant. Of course, not all hunters went to Africa. However, they could dream before the trophies pictured and the rounded ogive bullets like little artillery rounds. The Manufrance catalog is part of the perfect life of hunters in France. The company's demise was bitterly resented.

In 1855, Étienne Mimard and Pierre Blachon bought the French Firearms and Shooting Company from Martinier and Collin. They called their company the French Manufactory of Firearms and Bicycles at Saint-Étienne. The Ideal shotgun appeared in 1887; it was a high-class side-by-side and one of the first hammerless shotguns. A small catalog devoted to cycles also appeared; twenty thousand copies were published. In 1889, three hundred thousand stout catalogs were printed and sent free to all the hunters in France. Success was immediate. The catalog contained scores of game bags; leashes; countless lures and decoys; very high-quality firearms; gleaming cartridges; knives from all over; boots; hats; jackets; pants; summer, winter, and colonial suits; cane guns; and revolvers. Some brands will remain graven on the minds and hearts of French hunters: the Buffalo rifle, the simplex single-shot gun, the Ideal gun, and especially the legendary Robust, which is now being manufactured again.

The Robust gun, as the catalog specified, was "a solid firearm, well-balanced and comfortable on the shoulder. Its barrel is constructed perfectly, its range and accuracy beyond reproach. Its cross-bolt locking

The shotguns are hand-assembled by workers of international renown.

great names in hunting

Using lampblack to fit an action.

system is very strong and capable of handling all hunting powders." The manufacturer added that he conceived of this gun "with the purpose of selling it at the lowest possible price and having it replace all hammer shotguns, whether pin fire or center fire, which are still in use, even though they are totally outdated." This was a masterful business move.

At the outset, Manufrance introduced the Reina air gun for young hunters, the Rapid gun (a pump action), the Perfex gun (a three-shot semiauto), and the Falcor (an over-and-under hunting and trap gun). In 1970, Manufrance made 65 percent of all French shotguns. The enterprise had over three hundred seventy-five thousand square feet of space in its factories at Saint-Étienne. Every year it sent out twenty thousand tons of merchandise in France and throughout the world. A million and a half households received its catalog. It was glorious. However, difficulties arose in 1975: tooling hadn't kept up with technology. Sales sagged. Manufrance, Inc. went into receivership in 1979. In 1980, the premises were taken over. After an attempt at forming a co-op, the industry was once again in danger. On January 20, 1986, Jacques Tavitian, a local industrialist, acquired the brands, patents, and models of the French Manufactory of Firearms and Bicycles at Saint-Étienne, including the prestigious brands Manufrance and MF. It was a new start.

"A million and a half households received its catalog."

Equally attractive were the single-shot guns, the little garden guns, and the air guns.

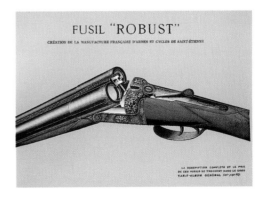

FUSIL "ROBUST"

More than a name—a legend! The Robust, the shotgun of rural hunters, is a good match for all climates.

The good old days when the fields weren't all under cultivation. There were more partridge and quail then, much to the satisfaction of the rural hunters.

Above: Cover of the book by Adolphe d'Houdetot.

Left: Hunters from the nineteenth century. Note the exterior-hammer gun, the large game bag, the gaiters, and the friendly gendarme who's there for the opening of the season. This was the black-powder era.

Adolphe d'Houdetot: With Pen and Gun

No book about hunting has had more impact than *The Rustic Hunter* (1847), which has been reissued in every possible format, on all kinds of paper, and always with rousing success.

The book's author, Adolphe d'Houdetot, surely had no idea he was going to make such a splash when he brought his manuscript to Charpentier Publishing in 1847. We don't know much about d'Houdetot except perhaps that he spent a good deal of time in the army. His military service prompted him to sign as "Adolphe d'Houdetot, Soldier." He described himself as follows in the foreword of the first edition: "I am a child of the bullet! I owned a gun at the age of twelve and was a soldier at thirteen; I didn't own so much as a spot of land, but I poached regularly whenever I could bribe the rural policemen with a fifty-cent piece, and a uniform button on a common coat got me in good with the honest and incorruptible gendarme. That's how I spent my youth."

Physically, he was—judging by a portrait from the period—a large, jolly fellow equipped with a mustache and a long nose that even he sometimes made fun of. Hunting was his passion. In contrast with what goes on today, where the meanest writer puts on airs and poses like someone really important, he hunted with humor and a detachment that are refreshing. He was a haphazard hunter who would beat the countryside with unreliable dogs, a broad-brimmed hat, a rustic shirt, leather boots, and a huge, fringed game bag. He would bring his lunch along. At midday, he would sit down at the foot of an oak to munch a hunk of bacon on a piece of bread. He would play with the game and recount his misadventures more than his exploits. Nevertheless, that didn't keep him from being a crony of Jules Gérard, the lion slayer, to whom he dedicated his book: "To you, brave Gérard." Jules Gérard was cut from different cloth. He was the one who put forth this idea: "To *have fun* with a lion, you need two players: the lion and you." Jules Gérard had a swash-buckling side. He gave us forceful and detailed descriptions of the

"He would play with the game and recount his misadventures more than his exploits. . . ."

Duck hunting. Punts drive the game toward a hunter concealed behind a willow tree.

You have to make close shots because the guns aren't that great. This hunter bowls over a rabbit right at his feet.

You don't get a chance to bag a boar like this one every day.

"tests of strength" that brought him into confrontation with the wild animals and from which he always emerged victorious, bloodied, of course, but still alive. On every page of his book, he commends his soul to God. There's none of that in d'Houdetot's writing. One writer was a poet; the other, a warrior. He also knew Bombonnel, "the panther slayer." That was the era when the first hunters, armed with long black-powder rifles, went to Africa to come up against wild animals. We can scarcely imagine d'Houdetot in these confrontations. He's more attracted to mild-mannered beasts: hares, partridge, and cottontail rabbits. He sees them as friends, describes their habits and their ruses, and has a good laugh when they outsmart him, which is often the case. *The Rustic Hunter* is a succession of stories studded with puns and other plays on words. There's a humorous side to our hiker of the plowed fields. The author is also very good at digressions outside of hunting. He constantly amuses himself as well as us. For example, here's how he describes getting a first gun. "There's a curious thing that happens in some households that goes something like this: 'Arthur,' says the mother to her seventeen-year-old son, 'if you win a prize I'll get you a gun on our next vacation.' Arthur is a studious young fellow; he at least gets a prize for having grown a lot and is given his first gun. And he respects the valuable saying that 'A gun that's unloaded is loaded for an accident,' which means that a cartridge may have been forgotten in the magazine. Also, 'There are three things that a wise person must never count on: favor from important people, the faithfulness of women, and . . . nice days in the winter, or even in the fall. Good advice for hunters and lovers.'" He makes some strange observations and notes that maintain that domestic turkeys make the best pointers: "When you're out hunting and you see some turkeys in a field purposefully surrounding a particular spot and making a certain clucking noise, you can be sure that they are pointing at a hare, a rabbit, a cat, or a marten." D'Houdetot also gives us some sage advice: "If you walk too quickly in climbing a hill, remember that you'll expend a lot of energy for nothing. If you ask a *native* of the Campan valley how long it takes to get to the top of the Pic du Midi, he'll answer, 'Four hours if you take it easy, and six if you hurry.'" *The Rustic Hunter* also plunges us into a sort of hunting paradise, when it was possible to hunt on the outskirts of Paris and when the game bag always had something in it. "On February 7," d'Houdetot reports, "I killed a quail in the vineyards of Argenteuil." At that time there were no game laws, and you could shoot practically anything you wanted to. So our friend hunted sea swallows, which are a type of tern. He notes that this

Above: The master gunsmith sights in a rifle.

Opposite: Hunting partridge in a cabbage field. Some nice coveys flush right in front of the dog's nose.

D'Houdetot has a bite to eat before setting off on new adventures.

"He really had a sentimental side!"

type of hunting is among the most enjoyable "as long as you don't feel that little heart beating a thousand reproaches in the pocket of your game vest." He really had a sentimental side! He would also go after guillemots on the cliffs of Etretat, marsh birds on the banks, and wood grouse in the mountains. He was also fanatical about hunting with hounds, which led him to write another book about hunting small game. He also wrote *Poaching and Anti-Poaching Measures*, a work that's doubly remarkable because the author excelled in both endeavors.

Oberthur in the Land of the Animals

A woodpecker and a squirrel, a mischievous encounter.

Although trained as a doctor, Joseph Oberthur (1872-1956) certainly spent as much time examining wild game with his artist's pencil as he did people with his stethoscope. He left an impressive body of naturalist work.

The good doctor could handle the stethoscope as well as the pencil. Oberthur's sketches are wonderful, for the expressions on the animals' faces go straight to our heart. Every hunter who sees his pictures of wildlife and game dogs immediately thinks, "That's perfect!" He had a photographer's eye. His paintings are not of the same quality as his drawings, though. Although less comfortable working in colors than with charcoal and pencil, Joseph Oberthur occasionally branched out into some extreme color prints. Just the same, in his depiction of positions and behaviors, he remains an incomparable master.

"He was fascinated by animal life. . . ."

When you open one of his books, the whole population of the woods, plains, and swamps leaps right out at you!

"I'm no erudite person, but I have always lived in a natural setting, and I have been a passionately devoted observer. For more than fifty years I have been filling up albums with sketches of animals I have seen, some fleeing or dying, and others in their regular daily life." That's how Joseph Oberthur introduces himself in his book *Wild Game in Our Country*. Some critics accuse him of imprecision in his texts and make fun of his "heroic" tales of hunting species that are protected today. However, that's losing sight of the fact that during his time, people thought differently. Hunting was considered a normal activity and part of the fabric of rural life, and nobody questioned its validity. In that context, Joseph Oberthur was far from being a shooter concerned only with results. He was fascinated by animal life and projected the image of a hunter who respected the equilibrium of nature. That's the way this enthusiast, this great artist was; but this passion was never used to the detriment of his observation skills or of a certain scientific detachment.

Teal and water rail. As an insatiable observer, Joseph Oberthur never went anywhere without his sketchbook.

Hunter, fisherman, naturalist: this man had all the skills and was as comfortable sketching wood pigeons as otters or an undisciplined pointer.

These pigeons really look as if they're about to take flight.

Captivating picture of tight-sitting partridge right in front of the dog's nose.

The artist had a flair for getting the postures just right. It makes you feel like you're right there.

Born in 1872, this doctor, who came from bourgeois stock in the city of Rennes, France, devoted his life to perfecting his artistic talent. He was the son and grandson of printers. He was surrounded from infancy by experts from around the world with whom his father and his uncle, great collectors of butterflies and beetles, kept up a long-standing relationship. As a gifted illustrator, Oberthur began filling up sketchbooks at the age of ten. Two years later, he produced a "natural history of the birds of Brittany," an interesting series of wash drawings done somewhat in the Japanese manner. He was a lefty, but he also used his right hand. He used pencil, watercolors, gouache, and oil on various surfaces such as paper, canvas, and walls. Since he was a passionate hunter, he quickly turned to describing animal life in all its manifestations and built up an accumulation of sketches.

Joseph Oberthur wanted to get to know all the aspects of his sport. When he finished his military service with the thirteenth Chambéry battalion of alpine hunters, he took advantage of an opportunity to go after game high in the mountains. Subsequently, he became familiar with hunting waterfowl and marine animals. He also became a devoted supporter of traditional hunting methods, notably dove hunting with nets and the famous snare hunts for thrushes in the Ardennes forest.

During the Second World War, aware of the treasure he had built up, he referred in a letter to "all [his] sketchbooks, the product of forty years of shooting and hunting with hounds, and hundreds of sketches and watercolors, realistic documents depicting animals and the landscapes whose loss would be for [him] irreparable." He was an amazing dilettante who still found time to direct a highly regarded neurological clinic in Paris and keep a hand in the family's publishing business. Even though he was interested in all facets of hunting, hunting to hounds remained his favorite. He ran boar with his wild griffons from Bretagne and never missed a chance to ride in the forests of Val de Loire. His powers of observation and his artistic skill produced some incomparable studies on

". . . he took advantage of an opportunity to go after game high in the mountains."

30

animal life—studies that even today can be of use to scientists. Antoine Reille, a well-known ecologist, noted in the pamphlet produced for the exposition of the artist's works at the Gien Museum: "It's remarkable that someone had the temerity to write at that time that a buck doesn't necessarily add an antler point after each shed. And academics certainly didn't make adequate use of the antler illustrations he was able to sketch from life as they researched antler development in cervids." With reference to birds, Antoine Reille added, "I think I have found rendered precisely in Oberthur's sketches the things that I have seen through my binoculars."

"He was interested in all aspects of hunting, but hunting to hounds remained his favorite."

When Joseph Oberthur died in 1956, he left a considerable body of work. First was the extraordinary collection *Wild Game in Our Country*, published in seven volumes from 1936 to 1961. This work was reedited in 1971 and should be read by all newcomers to hunting.

Then there's the astonishing collection *The Wonderful World of Animals* in twelve volumes (out of print), where the author uses his talents to describe dinosaurs before moving on to the "giants of underbrush and forest," the "large beasts and other carnivores," wild ducks and other web-footed creatures," and "woodcocks, snipes, and small wading birds." Still within the realm of hunting, he wrote *Hunting and Fishing* (memories and sketches; out of print), *Migratory Game Animals* (out of print), and *All of Camargue* (in collaboration with Tony Burnand). The artist remains highly regarded, and his books still sell briskly.

You can still turn up this book at used book dealers.

The expression on this poor dog shows all the distress in the world.

People speak of a *Périnet* in the same tone reserved for *Rolls-Royce* or *Purdey*. The brand is sufficient unto itself because of its great prestige. The competition is far behind and has never really been a source of uneasiness for this prince of hunting horns.

The Legendary Périnet Hunting Horn

While light and musical, the Périnet hunting horn has become the world standard among hunters. Some have tried in vain to copy it. It's inimitable, and it's passed on from generation to generation.

"The Périnet, introduced 170 years ago, remains ageless despite its long years."

Many types of hunting horn exist. The Périnet, introduced 170 years ago, remains ageless despite its long years. Périnet is to hunters and hunting horn aficionados what Stradivarius is to violinists. François Périnet, who worked for the famous maker Raoux, provider of hunting horns to the court of France, opened his own shop in 1829. Since then, the torch has been passed from generation to generation. It's a family business even if the heritage hasn't always been passed on in a direct line. Each time, the new proprietor has been careful to include the notation "successor to Périnet" in his trade name to show that the manufacturing secrets have been carefully guarded. Périnet's son-in-law, then the son-in-law's son, and then a certain Mr. Dhabit stepped up to the controls in succession. Between the two world wars, Maurice Valéry assured the permanence of the business, which he passed on to his two workers, Mr. Tutin and Mr. Cheval. Then the small business experienced a period of

Not machine tools, but very basic devices powered by lots of elbow grease.

Sounding the Périnet is a custom common to everyone who has become a master of the specialty.

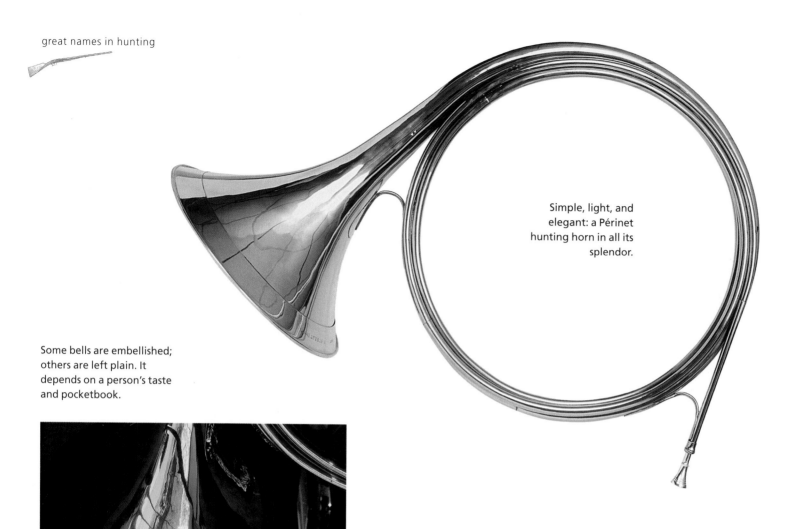

Simple, light, and elegant: a Périnet hunting horn in all its splendor.

Some bells are embellished; others are left plain. It depends on a person's taste and pocketbook.

The quality of the worker determines the quality of a good hunting horn.

turbulence, and the famous workshop set up at 40 1/3 Fabert Street was forced to close its doors. Michel Bureau, a boilermaker who had served his apprenticeship under the master artisan Cheval, acquired the business. Only after an evaluation that confirmed that his production was identical to the preceding one did an agreement, reached on November 20, 1967, authorize him to sign the hunting horns that he made at 174 Boulevard de Charonne as "François Périnet—Michel Bureau, successor."

In August of 1994, Yannick Bureau, the president's nephew, became the new successor to Périnet. He plays the hunting horn, as did his uncle Michel, and he established a number of hunting horn associations. He's the French basso champion and has been ranked in the highest category since 1975. In addition, he's the president of the Children of Saint Hubert, an association that's headquartered at the Hunting and Nature Center in Paris. Then the Périnet firm left its shop situated in Paris in the rear courtyard of the Boulevard de Charonne to set up shop under one of the sixty-five arches of the Viaduct des Arts in the twelfth precinct. The making of a Périnet hunting horn involves meticulous work. It's made

Forty hours of work and thirty thousand hammer blows are required to form a single instrument.

entirely by hand starting with a sheet of brass about 0.040 inches (0.3 millimeters) thick. The instrument is the product of about forty hours of work and thirty thousand hammer blows, including ten thousand just for the bell. The skills passed on through the generations and continually improved on are at the root of the company's success. It's what has allowed the brand to endure since the new instruments are identical to or even better than the ones that were used to sound the hunt in the early nineteenth century.

Industry has been able to produce some hunting horns that are much less costly than the Périnet. They are fairly light horns that are pleasant to sound. However, they'll never have the aura and the exceptional timbre of a hunting horn made entirely by hand. That's why as long as hunting lasts and devotees of the hunting horn exist, this specialty shop will continue to prosper.

"The skills passed on through the generations and continually improved on are at the root of the company's success."

Périnet, 71 Beaumarchais Boulevard, 75003 Paris. Phone: 01-42-04-03-39
Web page: www.perinet.fr

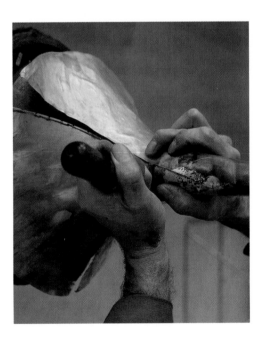

Making the bell entirely by hand from a sheet of very thin brass.

Gardeners dislike rabbits and hares because of their pronounced taste for cabbages. In this amusing nocturnal scene, the angry proprietor, still clad in his nightcap, takes aim at the intruders.

Hunting Illustrated: A Source of Happiness

T here are some magazines that no longer exist that we remember fondly in our hearts. Such is the case of *Hunting Illustrated*, subtitled *Life in the Country*. It achieved its greatest success at the end of the nineteenth century.

When created in 1867, this large-format journal aspired to be a meeting place for all hunters. The eye was immediately attracted to the nicely printed full-page engravings that represented spectacular or moving dramas: the death of a game warden or a poacher, a litter of pups in a basket, nuisance animals caught in a trap, setting out on opening day, hunting scenes in swamps, the charge of a tiger, and blinds bathed in moonlight. The content was a learned blend of scientific observations, adventure tales, opinions, various information, letters from the colonies, gossip, and classified ads. Take this one, for example: "Want to buy: large breech-loading duck gun for use in blind." It also contained information about horses, for at that time all hunters were also horse lovers. This was a weekly magazine that appeared every Saturday. Its title arched gaily across a frontispiece that depicted hunters, dogs, a deer about to expire, and fishing boats, for this hunting magazine was sometimes a magazine for fishermen, too. Its director was Mr. Firmin-Didot; a subscription cost thirty francs. The editorial offices of the journal were on Jacob Street in the sixth precinct of Paris. It was the meeting place of hunters, dog breeders, colonists returned from North Africa, artists, trappers, and the curious. The journal made a point of relating the picturesque hunting exploits of its readers. A letter from l'Aisne thus informs us that "the count de Brigode was hunting deer in the Folembray forest, and after three hours of pursuit, the animal tried to take refuge in the merchandise depot at the Rond-d'Orléans; dislodged by the mob, it tried to find hospitality with the mistress of the café in that depot, entered the pool room along with the fifty dogs that were chasing it, and was finally put down by the master huntsman, the Count de

"The journal made a point of relating the picturesque hunting exploits of its readers."

When taken by surprise when his dog breaks into a run, the unexpected flush of the woodcock, and a yawn, the unfortunate hunter can't even draw a bead on his intended game.

That was when no quarter was given to foxes, which were considered outlaws. This engraving shows a new misdeed.

Frontispiece of
Hunting Illustrated.

If you don't see it, you
can't shoot it! Keep
looking over there as
long as I'm around
here. . . .

This boy has just killed
the miscreant. His
good deed will be
rewarded.

Brigode. When the lady at the counter saw the new customer come in she fell into a faint."

Hunting Illustrated also aspired to bring together the different types of hunters and was glad to publish short announcements of the birth of a nice litter of dogs or the hatching of a covey of young partridges. Wolf hunting occupied a significant place, and the journal never failed to congratulate a hunting party or the leader of a wolf hunt who had rid the country of another animal. *Hunting Illustrated* didn't obey the canons of the contemporary press. It took its time; people chatted and drew things out. A report of some squirrel hunts, for example, filled a whole page with a continuation in the subsequent issue. The texts were sometimes embellished, but today it's the engravings that cause aficionados to swarm to sales rooms to buy collections of *Hunting Illustrated*. In fact, they have become worth their weight in smokeless powder. They told a whole story with a single picture, such as the unfortunate woodcock hunter who couldn't bag a bird because at the instant it flushed, he failed to suppress a yawn; or another entitled "Providing for the Empty-handed" that depicted a sheepish young hunter in the process of buying a few cuts from the poultry dealer.

Sometimes the tone was ribald, like the engraving that shows a pair of hunters attracted to two girls dozing at the edge of the woods and entitled "Fresh game?" Some scenes were charming; others were brutal; and still others were humorous, like the fox that had one duck pinned under its paws and didn't dare to let it go when a second one flew up in front of its nose. The label: "A bird in the hand is worth two in the bush. . . ."

Sometimes hunters make charming discoveries. . . .

"There was a certain philosophy of hunting at the end of the nineteenth century that emanated from every page."

There was a certain philosophy of hunting at the end of the nineteenth century that emanated from every page. First, people respected the game and hated poachers, whether two or four legged, such as foxes and winged poachers like birds of prey, which were trapped all year long.

Then the hunter of that time became ill at ease—already!—about the decline in game populations and pleaded for stricter regulations. Finally, he began to question the efficiency of his gun and his shooting, and he devoted lots of time to selecting the right dog. He spoke out in favor of truly wild game. As Ernest Bellecroix, a regular contributor, emphasized, "I have often repeated that ten chicks hatched in the wild, accustomed to the wild life and well acclimated, are worth far more than twenty chicks from a hatchery. If you share this opinion, you'll put a stop to the killing of your pheasants just as soon as you realize that you have just enough for the next season."

Excerpt from
HUNTING ILLUSTRATED

"If you want to have a good hunt using a decoy, four hunters should get together, not counting the boy whose job it is to make the decoy move.

Two hunters beat the field to flush the birds, which they shoot as soon as they get off the ground, while the two others stay close to the boy who pulls the string to move the decoy, which is the best place. To cook doves, skewer them and put them in front of a fire of burning twigs for seven minutes."

Frederick Courtenay Selous
(1851–1917).

The young man and his huge smoothbore, four-gauge gun.

Although injured many times, Frederick Courtenay Selous managed to pull through every time.

Selous: The Elephant Slayer

If the elephant were hunted today, it would not be the same as it was at the end of the nineteenth century, when the white hunters uncovered an immense country abundant in game and full of adventure.

"His record: twenty-two elephants with three guns in a single day."

The Englishman Frederick Courtenay Selous was one of the first mythical figures in deepest Africa. He was born on December 31, 1851 in London. At a very early age, he became a devotee of life in the wild. He set traps, fished for pike, and toughened up his body by swimming across the rivers in the English countryside in the winter. At age nine, he declared to his mother, "I'm going to be a hunter in Africa." While being educated at Rugby college, he wrote quite frequently to his family. Not to talk about his grades, but to ask them to send him slingshots. In spite of his passion for playing hooky, he finished his studies and contemplated becoming a doctor. However, he remained true to his vocation. On the fifth of September, 1871, he got onto a boat at Port Elizabeth. He had no personal fortune, so he could count on only his resourcefulness and his physical conditioning in facing the dangers of the bush. Fortified by his hunting experiences, he quickly became an expert tracker of lions and elephants. By selling ivory, he got enough money to launch expeditions with porters, horses, and oxen. He most often hunted from horseback, accompanied by dogs that saved his life several times. There was plenty of game. His record: twenty-two elephants with three guns in a single day.

Some period photographs depict this blue-eyed giant in the shade of a baobab, his head covered by a broad-brimmed hat, wearing a canvas shirt, pants, and leather boots. A large gash was visible on his cheek, the result of the heavy-caliber guns he used. He was fond of the gash, and every shot hammered it anew. He escaped death ten times, survived a concussion, and was caught in ambushes by rebel tribes but always managed to escape with his skin intact. Between African expeditions, he would return to London, where he was given a triumphal reception. He

The man and the beast, African version from the start of the twentieth century. Hunter and trackers strike a pose.

was unassuming by nature, and he returned to his first love, fishing, hunting, and watching the birds in the surrounding countryside. Although well liked by all, he made friends with Theodore Roosevelt, who also was a great hunter. Selous didn't refuse any invitations, except when they interfered too much with his habits. When someone suggested that they dine at the *Ritz* on grilled sole and a bottle of champagne, he responded, "No, thanks. I'm more partial to a slice of moose and a big cup of tea." The best gunsmiths of London gave him their latest guns, which he tried out in Africa by target shooting out the window of his bedroom. Despite progress in ballistics, he harbored fond memories of his two old four-bore guns with which he "killed seventy-eight elephants in three seasons."

"Between African expeditions, he would return to London, where he was given a triumphal reception."

Once he was in Europe, he thought about Africa, and vice versa. In 1915, at the age of sixty-four, he did everything he could to get into the army and go fight in Africa against the German expeditionary corps. Finally, he was accepted and made a lieutenant in a company of the French Foreign Legion. His colleagues included a former acrobat, a zookeeper, a general from Honduras, and a concierge, all of whom were "excellent fighters" in his estimation. He was promoted to captain but was killed by a bullet in the throat on January 7, 1917 at the head of his company 60 miles (96 km) south of Kissaki. He died as he would have wanted, on ground that he couldn't live without.

The buffalo is most fearsome when it's wounded and it charges out of the long grass.

Doctor Rocher: I Must Have My Ducks!

Scene from hunting from a blind. Three ducks dive toward the callers.

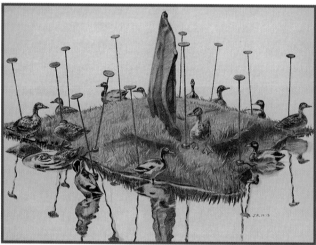

Decoys "resting" on a hummock in the Saint-Vincent swamp in Gironde.

"Surrounded by snipes at that time, and in the blinds!"

Doctor Rocher, the author of the book *Duck Hunting* (1953), remains one of the great figures of waterfowling. A man who dedicated his life to ducks, he left a body of work that in many ways was a premonition of things to come and that is still used for reference today.

"My dear friend and doctor,

I received your last letter [September 19, 1948] informing me of your trip to Paris on October 2. Unfortunately, you forget that we are hunters . . . and waterfowlers . . . . Surrounded by snipes at that time, and in the blinds! . . . . So I won't be able to be in Paris at that time. My apologies, my good doctor, for this unfortunate turn of events.

Best wishes, Viscount de Brossin de Méré."

This letter, written to Doctor Rocher by the owner of the very famous Blind of the Big Shots, may seem cavalier. It's not, because it's accompanied by the following postscript:

"Look. If you can, on Monday, October 4, take the train at 2:10 p.m. from the north station, headed for Boulogne-sur-Mer. Get off at Noyelles-sur-Mer at 4:40 p.m. We'll pick you up by car. Night flight at my blind, dinner, night in the blind, Tuesday morning, a little snipe expedition." Doctor Rocher didn't miss the chance. "One of the great dreams of my hunting life had just materialized," he wrote in the book that made him famous, "to be invited to the Blind of the Big Shots at Sailly-Bray by the proprietor."

That was an invitation that left nothing to chance. At that time, Doctor Rocher was already an uncontested champion duck hunter. His book entitled *Duck Hunting*, published in 1953 by Editions de la Toison d'or, furnished the proof.

His preface, which is written as a poem, ends like this:

Where all is calm
There are a thousand sounds of silence,
Close your shop window for a moment
And read this Book of Knowledge

Cover of Dr. Rocher's book.

Pintail ducks coming in; the long tail characterizes the species.

Slowly turn these pages
And remember that they are dedicated to you.

Fully five hundred pages long and beautifully illustrated by Boyrie, the book was published in Paris in 1953 by Toison d'or Publishing Company. The first edition consisted of a hundred and fifty copies. It's a seminal work—a reference book that covers waterfowl hunting and treats the techniques as well as the history. That's a history that goes back very far, for the authors actually delve into the Mesolithic age. Dr. Rocher in fact surrounded himself with several very talented historians and scientists, notably Professor Bourdelle, Professor Fabre, Mr. Mouchan, and the Count de Valicourt, a great name in waterfowl hunting. Each one of them spent hours collecting impressive documentation. The work became a great success and was quickly sold out. In 1977, a young editor from Bordeaux, Martiel Trollier, decided to reissue the book, which had been updated and revised by Dr. Rocher himself and his collaborators.

"A reference book that covers waterfowl hunting. . . ."

Pool by a blind at sunrise. An atmosphere of original purity.

Purdey: More than a Gun, a Legend

The gentleman's gun goes well with tweed, elegant luggage, and deluxe cartridges.

T he old building on South Audrey Street, with its old-style display windows, its columns, its woodwork, and its prim salespeople, continues to fascinate hunters all around the world.

Myths are durable. The Purdey image is highly resistant to tarnishing: as time goes by, it gets stronger. The brand is even known to people who don't hunt. It's synonymous with prestigious guns. Its royal origins and tremendous quality have earned worldwide renown for the old company on South Audley Street in London. Purdey was founded by Mr. James Purdey under the reign of King George III; he had decided to manufacture the best gun in the world. He assembled the best workmen, took his time, and made his dream come true. The gun quickly became the favorite of the royal families—in the European courts as well as in England—and of well-heeled explorers. In the Indies, British officers drew a bead on tiger after tiger using Express guns bought in London. In Europe, affluent hunters took to buying not one but two guns—a pair, or even a trio for use on some outstanding drives. That allowed for quicker shooting. Among kings, heads of state, prime ministers, and ambassadors, the Purdey became a highly valued gift.

Even today, buying a Purdey is almost like some ritual. You first have to be ushered into the *long room*, draped in red fabric, where the walls are adorned with numerous testimonials of gratitude from satisfied customers: princes from all the courts of Europe, industry magnates, and artists from the past and present. The walls are also lined with display cases containing the company's most beautiful pieces. This room is not open to everyone. You first have to prove that you make the grade and have an ample portfolio, for the guns cost the equivalent of a luxury car. Gentlemen clad in gray, very dignified, straight out of the Victorian era, gingerly emerge from the shadows. You talk for a long time, before a cup of tea, concerning gauge, stock woods, the future owner's measurements, his tastes, and how he likes to hunt. Before getting down to business, the

"Gentlemen clad in gray, very dignified, straight out of the Victorian era. . . ."

A company that has made lots of princes happy.

44

Fine engraving, high-quality wood, and flawless finish.

representatives bring out a blue-covered catalog that displays the few available models. Of course, all types of modifications are available. This catalog offers just two types of engraving: the "standard fine" of the *fine rose and scroll* type, "the kind most frequently used on our guns," and the Purdey *extra finish*, with more elaborate scrollwork. The work is sober but astounding in its detail. The engraving is actually done by great artists who work in small volume with no production requirements and who can spend hours reproducing minuscule designs. Purdey had to accept the changes in the marketplace and now offers over-and-under shotguns. These guns don't have as much charm as the traditional side-by-sides, but at least they're available and can be had in five gauges from 0.410 to 12. The future customer is requested to note that "making an over-and-under requires more time than the other guns and that delivery time will be longer."

"The engraving is actually done by great artists. . . ."

Concerning the maintenance of the guns, Purdey specifies that it's advisable to return them every year to the company for a complete checkup and that the cost of this operation is "astonishingly negligible" in comparison to the gun's value. In any case, when you buy a Purdey, it's like buying a Ferrari; you can afford to have the service done.

The brand that has become *the* standard among shotguns.

These gentlemen at Purdey, who look remarkably alike, are much as they would have been during the Victorian age.

AROUND THE WORLD

AROUND THE WORLD

What makes certain places magical? Why do you always return to them according to some almost ritual obsession? Simply because in those places, the ingredients of pleasure are mixed so perfectly that they become irresistible.

"And then there are all the adventurous hunters who take off with their nose to the wind. . . ."

Not all hunters are fixated on the same places. The big-game hunter looks to the great forests in the east of France and Europe, the waterfowler thinks of the bay of Somme, and the upland game hunter gravitates toward Spain or Poland. Woodcock hunters think only of the vast peat expanses in Ireland, a country that will never let him down. However, we also know of some flocks of wood pigeons that make a pilgrimage every summer to the pea fields of Great Britain. And then there are all the adventurous hunters who take off with their nose to the wind in search of new scents. Who cares if there aren't many birds and the shooting is unpredictable? What counts is the beauty of the countryside, the friendliness of the people, and the

regional customs. Just as a salmon fisherman knows perfectly well that he stands a chance of returning from Iceland empty-handed, a mouflon hunter can use up several weeks among the summits of Kashmir without the slightest chance of firing a shot. Everyone knows that you don't go to the Blind of the Big Shots with the idea of bagging a staggering number of ducks. In spite of its grandiloquent name, the famous blind is often a disappointment—from the mere standpoint of yield. However, every minute spent in this sacred place is an enchantment. It's as if the paneled walls were murmuring words of love, words of wind and feather, the words of a dream woven by hundreds of hunters who have pursued waterfowling here throughout the night. Another dreamy place is any territory where we got our start in our youth. We return with the joy we knew when we were twenty, and any game we take there is worth ten times as much as the equivalent taken anywhere else. That's the way men and hunters are. Emotion, memories, and even regrets mark them with an indelible seal.

From left to right:
Heading out to hunt Barbary partridge in the Atlas Mountains of Morocco.

Quail hunting in cropland near Taroudant, Morocco.

Retrieving a grouse in the French Alps.

Sunrise on the Iraty forest in the Atlantic Pyrenees. Will the wood pigeons make the appointed meeting?

Crotoy mud flats at low tide (northwestern France).

Gray lag geese and mallards on a pond.

The Glory of the Somme

This waterfowler has just bagged a mallard in perfect condition.

One of the favorite dreams that hunters have is to go hunting at least once in their lifetime in the Bay of Somme in northwestern France. That's because thousands of waterfowl are on those vast mud flats, and the sight is so impressive that even if you turn up empty-handed, you still are never bored.

An immense salt marsh where thousands of birds take flight: that's the Bay of Somme, a jewel of a hunting spot on the coast of Picardy. It's a flat land of almost 17,000 acres (6,800 ha) of greenery, water, or sand, depending on the stage of the tide, which rules the life of humans and animals alike. At low tide, as the ocean rises, it scarcely brushes the sandy edge of the salty meadows where flocks of sheep graze. At high tide, the water swallows everything and comes right up to the edge of the paved roads. The Bay of Somme lives for and by hunting. Everyone here gazes skyward when the migrations are on. Dozens of blinds stud the seashore. Blinds are visited every night during hunting season and carefully looked after during the off-season. There's no trifling with waterfowl here. Even the government realizes that hunting is an integral

A handsome winter teal at rest.

The indispensable Labrador doing its job.

Pierre Gérard, a major figure in the bay area.

part of the local tradition. The proof lies in the fact that the Museum of the Bird near Saint-Valéry de Somme has reproduced the interior of a hunting blind. The residents of the bay are passionately devoted to waterfowling. They practice it in countless ways: by the boot (while walking), in blinds, from shanties, by still-hunting, and from pop-up blinds. Hunting from blinds is the most popular technique. In one instance, a hole is dug in the sand and covered with a tarp to conceal the hunter. A variation involves the coffin or pop-up blind, an oblong box placed onto the sand and into which the hunter slips. These two techniques are used for shooting birds that are known as *demersal* or ocean birds. Only a few species are fair game; the others are protected.

The Bay of Somme is also a center for other types of hunting from blinds. In the evening, the hunter takes his place in a camouflaged shelter set up near a duck pond, where he places a set of decoys. The wild birds land next to them. Usually, the results are quite modest—an average of one or two birds per night—but the place has such a reputation that people come from all over France to spend a night in a blind. Four towns dot this natural curiosity. To the north is Le Crotoy, a fishing village that

A flight of oystercatchers heading for the mud flats.

A pair of quackers for the game bag. That's the idea. . . .

A flock of sheldrakes on the Bay of Somme. These protected birds are numerous.

has had its share of celebrities, including Colette and Jules Verne. It's said that this is the place where the latter first saw the famous green flash. At the back of the bay is Noyelles-sur-Mer. Located behind the levees and the retaining walls from the 1900s, this little city holds something unusual: the Chinese cemetery. This is where the remains of the unfortunate coolies lie, who were used by the English during the Great War. Still at the back of the bay is Saint-Valéry-sur-Somme and its medieval ramparts that surround the high city. Joan of Arc stayed here when she was a captive. She crossed the bay on horseback en route to her destiny. . . . Finally, to the south is Cayeux-sur-Mer, a whaling port with Belle-Époque villas. It stretches as far as the little fishing village of Hourdel. There's a scenic road that goes around the site. You can also take the little train that formerly served all these localities from Noyelles. Hunters pour in during the two or three days that follow the full or the new moon, when tides are high, to watch the sea rise against the pastures and dislodge the thousands of ducks and wading birds that graze there. At all times, plenty of game is available.

You can't even take a step in the bay without hearing the whistling of an oystercatcher. Thousands of these black-and-white birds with a coral-colored beak exploit the shellfish beds, which unfortunately are in decline. You can also see Eurasian curlews, plenty of sheldrakes, and bernacle and greylag geese during the cold snaps in February. This is paradise for seabirds, the beloved birds that people throughout the region wait and watch for and that contribute significantly to the area's reputation.

"Hunters pour in . . . to watch the sea rise . . . and dislodge the thousands of ducks. . . ."

Female common teal.

You can't enter the bay area without taking a tour of Marquenterre Park. This an ornithological park established in 1973 for the benefit of migratory birds. The Shoreline Conservatory acquired it in 1986 and entrusted its management to the Joint Commission for the Development of the Coast of Picardy. The Marquenterre Nature Society operates it. It's a remarkable system of wet lowlands, swamps, and canals that has attracted an increasing number of migratory birds. It consists of two different venues. The first, referred to as introductory, *displays captive birds to the visitors. The second, termed* observatory, *makes it possible for photographers and scientists to study the wild birds in their natural environment.*
Marquenterre Park is a marvelous ecological display window. Only the Zwin Park in Belgium is as interesting. The coming and going of the birds, with the Bay of Somme right nearby, is constant and frequently spectacular.

While walking around the blind in the morning, recovering ducks that have been wounded along the banks is common. The ducks come to seek refuge among the rushes.

Viscount Brossin de Méré devoted his life to hunting migratory birds, as his grave marker indicates.

The Blind of the Big Shots

A veritable house buried in the swamp, with bedrooms, dining room, smoking room, kitchen, bathroom, and observation deck: the pride of Viscount Brossin de Méré and the absolute dream for waterfowlers.

"The Blind of the Big Shots is a sort of yacht set onto the mud of a swamp."

You can follow your dreams to the very end. That's what the Viscount de Brossin de Méré did. In 1904, he had the Blind of the Big Shots constructed on the swampland of Sailly-Bray. It wasn't named that because the hunting success was so spectacular there but because his wardens had been instructed to fire four hundred shots into the air at the moment of its inauguration. This aristocrat, a passionate devotee of waterfowl, today reposes in the little cemetery at Noyelles-sur-Mer under a headstone decorated with ducks and woodcocks. The Blind of the Big Shots is a sort of yacht set onto the mud of a swamp. It's an immobile boat, but it shudders and creaks under the force of the west wind. The interior resembles that of a cruise ship, with its paneled ceiling that dishes into the observation deck, its portholes, its small rooms like staterooms, and the three steps at the entrance that allow you to climb on board. Ivy and climbing vegetation disguise the structure, which melts into the background. What refinement! There are a decoy pond the size of a swimming pool, a kennel, guest rooms, the viscountess's apartments, a boathouse, and even the famous *palace of the dead*, the screened-in closet where the victims of the hunt were hung up. Spending a night at the Blind of the Big Shots involves first and foremost paying homage to the memory of a waterfowler who was in love with hunting; it involves dreaming and basking in the wind and the memories. It's a good blind but little more. You can bag whistlers, teal, gadwalls, and an increasing number of graylag geese at the end of the season. The woodcock marsh is excellent in July and August, but it quickly becomes hard to work once the rain begins. You can frequently step into the water right up to your hips. That's why many hunters prefer to hunt in waders. When you flip through the record book, you see that the harvest has been quite modest:

The pond in front of the blind in all its splendor, with its screened-in decoys and the facility's perfect camouflage.

"You sense that the hunters came to collect themselves in this palace of water-fowling. . . ."

a duck here and there, two teal there, sometimes four or five ducks. The comments are never harsh. You sense that the hunters came to collect themselves in this palace of waterfowling; that they tasted the pleasure of being isolated in the unique framework of the marsh; that the passage of a few flights of migratory birds and the nostalgic sound of the duck calls were all they needed to be happy. Normally, you arrive at the blind after lunch. You hunt in the marsh during the afternoon, then you take in the evening pass before spending the night in the blind. At dawn the following day are the morning pass and another trip through the marsh. After many vicissitudes, the blind was purchased in 1991 by the Joint Commission for the Management of the Picardy Coast, whose primary shareholder is the general council. Today, it is available for rent. And anyone can, with a year's lead time, spend some time in this amazing conservatory of waterfowl hunting.

Setting a live decoy at the edge of the pond.

Left: At water level, like the Eskimo in his kayak, the hunter has the strange sensation of floating in the middle of the current. He sits up only to shoot.

Above: The guide sets the decoys, gets the client set up, and then camouflages himself on the shore.

Above and right: The decoys are much bigger than real life, undoubtedly so that the game can see them better. Setting out several dozen around the blind is common. Their position depends on the daily wind conditions.

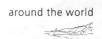

"Current Events" on the Saint Lawrence

Eyes at water level, head among the stars, the waterfowler can experience a dream come true in the blinds of Quebec.

Myriads of ducks flutter above the frigid waters of the Saint Lawrence River in Quebec. The hunters there have perfected a special hunting technique that gives you the strange sensation for a couple of hours of being an atom in the middle of a river, where you can scarcely see the two banks. It involves a strange type of punt, almost more like a buoy, as French waterfowlers would call it. Everything gets under way at dawn. You get into a boat propelled by a huge outboard motor. The boat tows the buoy behind it; it's sort of like a flat barge with a hole bored through it. On the sides are two arms that hold a bucket. A lever is used to lower the bucket into the opening and down into the water. There's room inside it for 200. They sit on a bench and brace their legs against the walls, with their eyes at surface level. For the barge is amazingly flat—so flat that it's fitted with a type of skirt that protects the men from the spray. Once they get to the middle of the river, the guide anchors the barge, drops the bucket into place, gets his clients set up, and leaves. He stops some 200 yards (180 m) away so he can come and see what's happened as soon as he hears shots. His job is to pick up the dead and wounded ducks. Before leaving the hunters, he carefully sets out a couple dozen wooden decoys around the barge. Some are as big as a goose. Evidently, the ducks can see them more clearly. As soon as the motorboat leaves, silence returns to the liquid expanse. All you hear is the sound of the wind and the splashing of the waves against the hull. Day breaks slowly. Dawn imparts a blush to the waves.

While bundled up in camouflaged and quilted outfits, the hunters curl up and wait for the migrating birds. Some of them fly over high in the sky, but others appear even with the waves, in other words at eye level. These are primarily divers, common pochards, and tufted ducks.

"As soon as the motorboat leaves, silence returns to the liquid expanse"

Sunrise on the river. . . and on the chilled hunter.

To buck the current, the guide uses a boat with a powerful motor.

The birds occupy a home range where everything possible is done to make things comfortable for them.

Hunters and *secretarios* hasten to the stands.

The best ranges are located in the center of Spain.

The Brave Partridge of La Mancha

Bare, ochre expanses where you experience dense flights of red partridge as brave as the local bulls—that's what keeps things interesting.

". . . and you have to shoot with two or three guns."

Hunting the red partridge is an institution in Spain. The best shotgunners in Europe meet there for the sumptuous hunts that bring together dozens of beaters. The partridge are always guaranteed to be wild. In fact, they are raised in masses but in the fresh air. It's the same technique that's used for the great pheasant hunts. Red partridge are grown and fed on thousands of acres; they're given shelter in areas that have been rid of predators. The birds aren't entirely wild, to the extent that they're pampered by humans. However, they don't pop out of a box and fly in a straight line. These are brave partridge.

When you walk behind the scenes at these exceptional hunts, you literally push a moving walkway of partridge ahead of you. The fact is that lots of birds are needed, when you consider that every day three hundred to seven hundred fowl are taken in the course of five or six hunts. The hunters are situated behind straw blinds while a long line of beaters pushes the game to them. At each end of the line, a horseman directs the operation. You have to wait a good twenty minutes, sometimes a lot longer—it all depends on the area where the drive takes

The birds take off as if they were shot from a cannon. The best shotgunners in the world get together for these hunts.

Each shot requires lots of concentration. As soon as you let up, you start to miss, much to the chagrin of the hunters.

On a hunt, bagging a dozen partridge is easy.

"The hunter is aided in his task by a man known as a secretario."

place—before the birds start to appear. Then the pace of fire becomes frantic, and you have to shoot with two or three guns. The hunter is aided in his task by a key man known as a *secretario*. His job is to spot where the birds fall so he can pick them up at the end of the drive. He applies himself to this task with all the more diligence because he knows full well that the size of his tip depends on the size of the take. Once it's announced that the hunt is over, the *secretario* gambols like a lamb as he rushes to collect the game. He doesn't use half measures, and casts his net wide; and if he can round out his booty by scooping up some of the take from the adjacent stand, so much the better!

This hunt gathers together the elite wingshots from throughout Europe, who come here to challenge one another in what sometimes resembles a real competition. The Spaniards aren't left out. They manage to bet some considerable sums of money among themselves, somewhat like the days when live pigeon shoots were permitted. All that in a sumptuous setting, with mountains, horses, and luxury all-terrain vehicles. In short, you're in well-heeled company. The itinerant hunters have their rites: grouse in Scotland in August, pheasants in England in October, and red partridge in Spain a little later. That's their idea of the good life.

Windmills dominate the hilltops of la Mancha.

Above and right: The British are past masters in the art of organizing high-flying pheasant drives. The gunners are placed far enough from the woods to force the birds to pass very high. That's what makes the English drives so charming.

While sporting Barbour vests and tweed caps, the guards, accompanied by Labrador Retrievers, assure efficient service.

High-flying Pheasants in Search of Gentlemen

A wool garter keeps the socks from falling down.

A pheasant is good; an English pheasant is better. After all, one mustn't mistake the fowl from Sologne for the rockets that zoom across the misty skies of Norfolk.

The British prefer playing games to hunting. When they hunt to hounds, they make royal fun of the fox, the main object being to have a good sport as they jump the hedges one after another. The more they change foxes, the better the outing. In fact, one can just as well replace the fox with a fox skin dragged across the ground. That's called a *drag*, and it's a source of amusement for every good horseman. They apply the same spirit to pheasant hunting. Whereas a French hunter rejoices at the idea of downing a bird that jumps up from between his feet and that will be great roasted, the Englishman experiences different emotions. The pheasant becomes like a billiard ball, and the fun is in setting up some good, difficult, three-cushion banking shots, that is, high-flying triples. For that purpose, he raises hundreds of pheasants on hundreds of acres according to the proven technique of the English aviary. Young birds are placed in screened enclosures of several acres. When they learn to fly, they can get out. However, they'll come back, attracted by the good grain that they're provided with at all hours of the night and day. From their infancy, the pheasants live outdoors and therefore behave just like wild birds. The only problem is that they are flighty. So the trick is keeping them where they belong. They are chained by their stomach, so to speak. The areas are patrolled regularly by an all-terrain vehicle so that the prodigal offspring can be returned to the fold.

"The British prefer playing games to hunting."

The hunters on the drives are situated in extreme conditions—such as at the bottom of a ravine—so that the shooting is difficult. They will also be stationed far from the edge of the woods so that the fowl don't run up to their feet. When they leave the premises, the hunters are supposed to be able to say to themselves, "Ah, what beautiful birds!" or "Ah, what great birds!" Those are the hallowed phrases. If the organizer doesn't hear them, he's disappointed. Great quantities of cartridges are expended, and a take of six hundred birds with eight guns doesn't cause anyone to raise an eyebrow. All that with absolute professionalism and a sense of a job well done.

In certain hunts, only the cocks are taken in order to permit the game to regenerate. A pox on the gunner who draws a bead on a hen!

Setting out on a warthog hunt at dawn, the moment when the bush wakes up. The sun suddenly appears, the insects resume their stridulations; it's a magic moment.

Hunters in Africa

The guide plays a pivotal role in a warthog hunt.

"There you hunt big game with a guide. . . ."

Immense expanses trembling in a fog of heat, dangerous animals, and the scent of adventure continue to make this destination a rite of passage for hunters from all around the world.

There's something unique about hunting in Africa because of the framework in which it takes place. It's not just a continent but another planet that obeys its own laws and imparts incomparable emotions to anyone who travels there.

Africa hides its share of drama: hunters lost in the bush and dead of thirst or wounds. There you hunt big game with a guide whose role is not to find the animals—he leaves that work to his trackers—but to protect his client. That means that in case of a charge, he has to be capable of dropping the animal instantly. The water buffalo, the lion, and the elephant are all potentially dangerous game. They're docile when they're left alone, but they can become killers as soon as they're wounded. That's also what gives these safaris their flavor, where in the space of a couple of seconds you can face a life-and-death situation. Of course, fatal accidents have become very rare. However, just knowing that the risk is there adds spice to the adventure. Hunting the large antelopes is more peaceful. Even though they can be dangerous when they're wounded, they still

You never go hunting
without a guide.

A hyena, a sneaky
scavenger of the bush,
left its tracks here. You
rarely see the animal.

This male warthog was killed in Senegal after a four-hour hike. It was high time!
The heat was becoming unbearable. Pretty impressive tusks.

don't have the fury of the large wild animals like the water buffalo and the elephant. Big-game hunting still goes on today despite the conflicts that bloody the African continent. People hunt in Cameroon, the Central African Republic, Burkina, Zambia, Botswana, Natal, Namibia, and Transvaal.

Small-game hunters also get their fill, whether it's a question of shooting ducks in Chad or francolins, a type of partridge, and turtledoves in Senegal or in Guinea-Bissau. The rhythm of these hunts is constant: get up very early in the morning, hunt for the francolins in the fields near the villages, return to camp for lunch. Siesta until around four o'clock. Then some pass shooting for grouse around a watering hole. Then pass shooting for sand grouse—birds that live in the steppes—around the same water hole at the start of nightfall.

During this visit, you'll cut your teeth on big-game hunting by going with a tracker to shoot a warthog. Hunters who have experienced Africa can never forget it. They remember the scent of the spices, the silent flight of the vultures over the bush, the sound of the drums in the villages at night, the noise of the generator, which goes off every night around eleven o'clock, and the dozens of colored birds that dart among the trees and transform the countryside into an Eden. And once they leave, they can think of just one thing: going back.

Tame female harnessed bushbuck in a hunting camp in Senegal.
A representative animal with its white stripes on the back.

Roissy: Rabbits Under the Jets

The presence of jumbo jets doesn't disturb the rabbits in the least.

It's a strange sensation to hunt bunnies a stone's throw from a 747 taking off from a runway at Roissy Airport, near Paris - especially if by some miracle a dog passes unharmed between the wheels of the huge plane.

"... these animals don't even run away when a plane goes by."

It's often said that our advanced civilization is incompatible with wild-life. In large measure that's true. Concrete, draining of swamps, the destruction of hedges, and the proliferation of pesticides have struck a hard blow against wildlife. Thank God, though, nature has a strong constitution, and lots of species adapt surprisingly well to their new environment. This is especially noticeable in the large airports where animal life prospers in spite of exceptional pollution and the deafening roar of the jets. The next time you take a plane, look out the window as you roll down the runway. You'll see gulls, hares, dozens of wild rabbits, Eurasian kestrels, starlings, plover, sometimes even some curlews, partridge, and geese. Undisturbed by the kerosene fumes and the decibels, these animals don't even run away when a plane goes by. In certain places, notably Roissy Airport, the airport authorities are even obliged to set up devices to scare the birds away. When birds get sucked into the jets, the consequences can be very severe. Even if these incidents don't jeopardize the plane, the physical damage is quite severe. People first tried to scare the birds away by calling in falconers. The experiment came to a sudden end. Today, audio recorders are used that imitate the alarm cries of the various species. Just the same, more energetic measures are often called for – especially because certain species, such as rabbits, don't react to the deterrent sounds, and they end up as roadkill on the accesses to the runways. Several thousands of these rodents are captured every year at Roissy, but despite this toll, there's no decline in the species. To stem what has become a veritable scourge, hunts are conducted.

When it senses danger, the animal hunkers down in the grass.

An unaccustomed sight: hunters on the tarmac at the Roissy-Charles-de-Gaulle Airport. The hunts are supervised by the police and regulated like clockwork.

The dog obediently follows on the heels of its master. He has to keep from getting under the wheels of the aircraft. That discipline is essential!

Every year, two thousand rabbits are taken at Roissy. They are released on club grounds all across France.

Above: The imposing profile of the Château de Chambord emerges from the smoke of a wood fire.

Right and far right: Reporting in at the château during a hunt; the guests are supervised by the local authorities.

Chambord: The National Wild Boars

S umptuous hunts for official hand-picked guests who spend the most beautiful hours of their hunting life here. "To be or not to be among them" is the persistent question that comes back to haunt the minds of everyone who for one reason or another has hopes of being invited to Chambord.

That's because the density of the boar population on these grounds, formerly royal but now republican, is really phenomenal. Several hundred are killed every year in prestigious hunts that bring together the upper crust of various political and diplomatic associations. Behind a stone wall 19 miles (31 km) long that was begun at the end of the reign of King François I, the Chambord national area contains a small village and, especially, the most vast and sumptuous château of the Loire Valley. It exists for us in the form that François I had envisioned. It has belonged to the state since 1932. Yearly it attracts a million and a half visitors, of whom eight hundred thousand go into the château.

"Several hundred are killed every year in prestigious hunts. . . ."

The state keeps up the hunting tradition of the area by maintaining an oak and pine forest and running controlled hunts for big game in general and for wild boar in particular. The hunts are controlled since, theoretically, hunting is not allowed in the reserve. So the guests act as administrators by getting rid of the most intrusive wild boar. And what boar they are! There's a real parade of these animals from which the guests can choose, and they'll never have another chance in their life to do so much shooting. It's easy to understand their enthusiasm when they walk through the gates of the reserve. The area is then cordoned off by the police and wardens in full dress uniform who officially salute the vehicles as they go by. Deputies, ministers, statesmen, high officials, foreign dignitaries, and a few members of the press are among the chosen. Michel Charasse used to be a regular. He would smoke a cigar between two hunts and tell jokes to his neighbors. Former French President Valéry Giscard d'Estaing had his customs, too. The hunt is conducted by

Boar at bay. The dogs hold it tightly until the hunter arrives.

The dogs have to be brave to stand up to an animal that can be dangerous once it's wounded.

Boars love water and mud, and they are quick to loll about in these two elements.

The underbrush is rolling in wild boar. Great populations are needed to satisfy the guests. In addition, Chambord is an internationally known showcase for hunting.

Two hunters drag a respectable boar toward the access road. At that point, all-terrain vehicles will transport it.

Well-defined boar track left in the moist ground.

There are numerous herds of boar; the animals are almost as prolific as rabbits.

In mid-September, the cry of the male deer—bugling—is the most distinctive manifestation of the mating season. All the woods resound with these raucous calls. The bucks show their mettle and size one another up by their voices, but we don't understand their language. The voice of the oldest male is usually the deepest, but voice alone is not a reliable indicator of the animal's age. The mating calls are a wonderful spectacle that attracts many curious onlookers. The officials at Chambord park have put together a very interesting program so that people can observe it. While accompanied by a forest warden, a group of no more than eight people can watch the bucks in the very heart of the reserve. And a large gallery that overlooks a prairie can accommodate several dozen people. The people who attend are passionately devoted to animal life; they include hunters, photographers, and naturalists. However, you have to reserve your spot long in advance, for the spectacle is a sellout.

the local officials with the aid of the wardens, beaters, and dog handlers. There are five or six hunts each time, highlighted by a brilliant presentation of the whole scene to the sound of hunting horns and torchlight. The spectacle is even more royal because of the many deer that bound away and are not hunted.

"Five or six hunts each time, highlighted by. . . ."

The hunters are stationed at the edge of the woods, either behind brush blinds or perched on small, elevated stands. After each hunt, all-terrain vehicles come to pick them up and deliver them to other stands. Everything is rather good-natured despite all the protocol, and it gives the wardens a chance to show off their expertise.

A German Short-haired Pointer on point. The bird is about to fly. This is when the hunter's attention needs to be clearly focused.

This woodcock fell into a puddle, as if in a display window.

Rambling on the Bogs of Ireland

C onfined in the ancient peat quarries, the Irish woodcocks give their pursuers a hard time. That's one of the reasons that they like that country so much.

"The bogs are former peat quarries."

What wonderful woodcock hunting they have in Ireland! Free of restrictions, or nearly so, cheap, and always filled with emotions, even if it's not always productive. For over there, sometimes you miss it. "They were here yesterday, but they left today" is still the watermark of this odd type of hunt. Where to go? There are simply too many choices, from the swamps of Shannon to the bogs of Kerry and Donegal. The bogs are former peat quarries – vast rolling spaces cloaked in fog and patches of black, with some nice green grass here and there that comes up to your groin. Woodcocks are most commonly hunted over bird dogs. Irish Setters and pointers are most commonly used. The main thing is the animal's ability to dominate the bird. Hunting woodcocks over bird dogs is surely the most exciting way to put birds into the game bag. Even if the dogs in Ireland aren't the most beautiful, their intelligence and their fighting spirit make up for that shortcoming. A large bird dog such as a pointer doesn't put up with a restricted territory. In Ireland, he's in his element. These dogs need plenty of room. They were bred that way, expressly to work large areas. A good dog has to stay away from the haunts of the wading birds. It has to resist all that, block out the inappropriate scents, keep its head up, follow the game, and come to a solid point. That's a lot to ask for! In Ireland, a hunter fairly commonly has to give the dog a push with the toe of his boot when the dog becomes transfixed by a bird that took flight for parts unknown a whole minute earlier.

"The main thing is the animal's ability to dominate the bird."

However, it's a rare pleasure to hunt with a gun dog that has a good nose, sound judgment, and experience. And you can find plenty of this pleasure on the Emerald Isle.

Vast expanses of peat, tufts of gorse, and a tireless guide. . . .

Wood Pigeon Mountain

Some stands are set up in the lower branches of the beeches in the Iraty Forest.

The Pyrenees Mountains in the morning light of a beautiful fall day.

The mountain passes in the Pyrenees have names from all over the world. Tharta, Sensibil, Millagate, Organbideska: magic names that evoke the exceptional days afield where the blue tide of wood pigeons flows on forever.

"Everyone who has ever experienced the blast of air on his cheeks that this bird produces. . . ."

People come to Saint-Luc, in the French Pyrenees, from all over Europe. And they wouldn't miss this week in October for anything in the world, for anything is possible. Shotgunning in the passes of the Pyrenees is a hunter's dream. Everyone who has ever experienced the blast of air on his cheeks that this bird produces can think of just one thing: going back up onto the mountain. Here the game is the wood pigeon, or the ringdove, as it's known on the other side of the Garonne River. However, the hunters spend more time watching the vultures soar in circles and the gyrations of the jays than they do seeing the pigeons. The migration depends on the climatic conditions and the direction of the winds. When the Pyrenees are blocked, no birds get through. And the hunters keep hoofing it . . . sometimes for days on end. The villages have figured out

72

A Prolific Bird

The wood pigeon—known as the ringdove in the southwest of Europe—is a prolific bird that hatches two or three broods per year. It's considered a nuisance in England, where it is hunted all year long. Every year, about three hundred thousand wood pigeons migrate through the passes, and the hunting harvest amounts to about 2 percent. The migratory routes have changed, and nowadays there are fewer birds than there were a decade ago. Just the same, some pleasant surprises occur, such as eighty thousand wood pigeons in one place in a single day during the 1999 season.

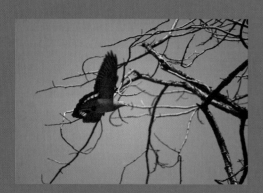

You have to be a bit of a mountaineer to venture into the mountain passes of the Pyrenees.

"The flock swirls around, hesitates, climbs, descends, and suddenly heads for the stand. . . ."

how to make money on the hunters. They have constructed roads and brought in fill. The hotels are full, and the gun shops can't keep the shelves stocked. Generally, the hunters set up shop in the *cayolars*, stone shelters put up for the shepherds who work in the area. It's a humble setup: one room, maybe two, partitioned for sleeping, a frying pan, a spring-fed basin, a table, and a few chairs. The day unfolds in a changeless ritual: at six o'clock in the morning, you get up and have some coffee. Then the hunters stick their heads outside and check the sky. If no clouds are visible and the wind is from the south or the east, the day may turn out to be a good one. They take their stands. The stands may be on the ground or built in the fork of a beech tree. These are rather improvised installations made of planks and camouflaged with netting or branches.

Then all the hunters have to do is scan the sky with binoculars to spot the birds. Long hours pass by. Then, suddenly a flight of wood pigeons appears. There may be a dozen birds or a whole flock containing hundreds, if not thousands, of birds. The flock swirls around, hesitates, climbs, descends, and suddenly heads for the stand. You have to exercise discipline and let the scouts go by—they sometimes fly too high—and shoot the last pigeons, for they are the lowest ones. Fog is the enemy of the wood pigeon hunter. You can see it rise from the valley. It creeps in on long tongues along the rock faces, slips among the trees, and swallows you up. Soon you can't see a thing at ten paces. You have no choice but to return to the *cayolar*. The migration will stall for days. The men play cards, read, simmer tasty meals of wood pigeon stew, pâtés, and broiled meats—all cooked in local wines. People come to the mountains for the ambiance as much as for the hunting.

Tired after a long stalk, this hunter from Bordeaux points with his cane to a flight of wood pigeons.

To loosen up their legs, some hunters sling their guns over their shoulders and hike in the woods in search of cèpe mushrooms, a thrush, or a stray wood pigeon. In the distance, you can hear the grumbling of a river. After a certain time, the fog shreds itself to pieces. You can make out a patch of blue sky, and the weather forecasts brought in on transistor radios start to sound more encouraging. Everything becomes possible once again, for the big flights generally occur after days of fog. The wood pigeons, which haven't been able to get through the passes because of the visibility, have backed up in the valley, where they have gorged themselves on acorns. As soon as the fog dissipates, they storm the peaks. Witnessing a huge flight is a privilege in any hunter's life. Thousands of birds pass through without a break. The air is filled with burned powder, and you hardly have time to reload. Birds fly through at all altitudes, some at ground level, others above the stands, and still others quite high in the sky. These exceptional flights last only a couple of hours.

"As soon as the fog dissipates, they storm the peaks."

A bird hung on the wall of a stand. Camouflage is very important, for the birds have sharp eyesight.

Above: At nightfall, the birds cluster around water holes, roosting on low branches. The wood pigeon is as numerous in Morocco as it is in Senegal.

Right: The passing flights also occur near the orange plantations, where the game rests as soon as the sun dips below the horizon.

Left: Shooting is very difficult, especially in the wind when the birds fly in a more unpredictable trajectory.

Turtledoves Under the Umbrella

T urtledoves fly fast. Wings folded back against the body, head pulled back, taking advantage of the slightest breeze, their flight takes a strange trajectory. That's why hunters like them!

The turtledove is easily recognizable by its narrow collar.

Turtledoves are capricious, light, unpredictable; they twirl rather than fly. That's why hunters value them so highly. However, late seasons make finding these birds in France hard nowadays. That's why you have to go to Morocco with its orange plantations. Of course, you have to observe the bag limits so you don't interfere with the birds' regeneration. We are steeped in anthropomorphism. Drawing a bead on a wild boar doesn't bother anyone since they're hairy beasts; but some hunters have reservations about turtledoves. Symbol of conjugal love, cherished by young women in antiquity, this graceful member of the pigeon family is associated with Venus. The ancients considered it to be a sacred bird, and Xenophon claims that it was protected in Syria. In Assyria, eating a turtledove was a serious offense. However, the turtledove is a prolific

". . . along the roads and the wadis, in the middle of the fields, there's nothing but cooing and the beating of wings."

bird that produces three broods every year. That's why it's considered a nuisance in Morocco and can be hunted starting in the month of June. And considering all the birds that flutter over the wheat fields and the desperate attempts of the fellahs to scare them away, having some regulated hunts seems reasonable. You have to walk in the vicinity of Agadir, near the orange plantations and in the grain fields, to get an idea of the amazing populations of the birds. In the eucalyptus hedges, on the trails, along the roads and the wadis, in the middle of the fields, there's nothing but cooing and the beating of wings. Like clouds of locusts, the turtledoves swoop down onto the fields.

This really isn't hunting—which presumes a difficult search for game— but it's difficult shooting. If the wind comes up, the birds play with the gusts in unpredictable ways. They swerve, climb steeply, hesitate, take off again, and hook back. This exercise takes place in the morning or the evening pass when the birds, which have gorged themselves on grain,

The hunt attracts a number of children who are happy to take advantage of the spectacle.

Given the number of spectators, you have to keep your shots high and avoid getting suckered in by a low-flying bird.

Excerpt from
THE MEANING OF HUNTING
by Jean Castaing

"And do you remember that pair of turtledoves? It furrowed the sky over the peaceful countryside and alighted on a poplar. The couple chose the same branch, and there the lovers, joining their beaks, half unfolded their quivering wings and tasted the joy of living and the sweetness of loving. One after the other, they passed right over your head. It would have been a great shot, but you missed the double. Didn't the long, desperate cry punctuated by the soft thud that ended the nuptial flight bother your ears? Well, perhaps you didn't hear it. I was only a few steps away and nearer than you to the spot where it fell; that's probably why that strident whistling. . . . Of course if I had fired too, I wouldn't have been able to hear."

return from the fields to spend the night in the orange trees. The weather is hot. While dressed in light canvas and a pair of hiking boots, with a container of a hundred cartridges at his feet, the hunter awaits the arrival of the birds. Some hunters sit on folding chairs, and others bring along an umbrella. The turtledoves arrive singly or in small groups, sometimes flying high in the sky, and sometimes only as high as a man's head. That's why you need to keep your composure. And from the start of the operation, you are surrounded by a cluster of impish youngsters whose enthusiasm and lack of discipline don't make the shooting any easier. Every cactus, every tuft of spines, every bush can hide a curious kid. So you have to keep your shots high. Most of the French, British, American, Greek, and Italian hunters who have come for a good time in Morocco understand that point.

At the start of June, before the concentrations of turtledoves newly arrived from deepest Africa have the time to scatter, the days of hunting are at their hottest. There are some spectacular arrivals in the Sous Valley, some flights that could cause a heart attack in hunters who live only for this little, wild, blue game bird.

A reasonable hunter mustn't get carried away by this hurricane of feathers but keep a cool head. There's no choice but to impose a limit on the number of cartridges. Instead of shooting everything and anything, and especially the easy birds, Saint Hubert, the patron saint of hunters, will be appreciative if the hunter targets only the most difficult ones. The turtledove deserves respect, and even if its meat is very fine, that's no

Helping a hunter by picking up downed birds: chances to earn a small tip that's always appreciated.

justification for filling the game bag to the top. Besides, the Fish and Game Department, as we have already pointed out, has set a daily bag limit in a well-directed effort to dampen the dove fever.

This type of hunting is very enjoyable since it takes place after the summer and winter hunting seasons in France. It's sort of a third time-out with its convivial yet truculent warm weather. You don't get frustrated because you miss a turtledove, unlike a woodcock, which is another matter altogether. Just as a soccer player rarely misses the upper corner of the net in a penalty shot, dove hunters often score a hit. However, you must never get too cocky. In this demanding type of shooting, a hunter may sometimes miss two shots in a row. Even a good shooter may suddenly lose the touch. He may miss one bird, then another, and then a third. Then, with or without turtledoves, you'll see him put on a more somber face. If the wind comes up at all and our shooter can't get back on target, the fireworks turn into a real fiasco. The shooting requires composure and steadfastness. Since small game is becoming rare in France and other western nations and putting up even a single bird often takes lots of effort, turtledove hunting in Morocco is really refreshing.

Turtledoves are a fragile game bird that's fairly easy to knock down with a charge of number-nines. However, you have to avoid excesses and be content with a modest take so the populations don't suffer.

This local pointer
of uncertain
origins has plenty
of enthusiasm and
doesn't balk at
the task.

The gallinaceans
love the alfalfa
fields – a treat for
this Brittany
Spaniel that reaps
the fruit of its
efforts.

The guides are
very adept at
finding the dead
birds even in the
thickest
vegetation.

Brittany Spaniel at work.
Was my retrieve
satisfactory?

The Quail of Taroudant

Morocco's rich Sous Valley, near Taroudant, is a favorite biotope for migratory birds. You can hunt here like in the good old days, behind a pointer, munching an occasional orange, one eye on your helper and the other one on the snow-covered summits of the Atlas Mountains. Now there's a dream. . . .

A string of quail harvested in the Taroudant region. A lot of hiking is needed to bag this game.

Rotund, dense, lively, and exquisite, the quail has provided hunters with many delicious meals. After some significant declines in population, the quail are coming back some, but the populations are nothing like the golden years of the 1960s, when bagging ten or a dozen birds in a morning was common enough. Nowadays, you're lucky to get two or three a day in prime territory. And that takes a fair amount of luck. That's why hunters who like the real thing are so fond of going to Morocco and, more specifically, to the plains of the Sous Valley, near Taroudant. The game populations are satisfactory, the guides are dedicated, and at least in theory, the weather is mild. And what about the dogs, you may ask. What dogs they are! Sure enough, hunting quail without a dog is like smoking a dry Havana cigar—half the pleasure is gone.

Here it seems that the pointers have shrunk a little in the sun, and the Brittany Spaniel has a peculiar little face. However, these dogs are hunters, and that's what really counts. Short, thin, and muscular, they are athletes who can beat the bush all day long without slacking the pace. As a backdrop, there are the Atlas Mountains, often blanketed in snow at the end of the year, and at your feet, produce gardens: potatoes, tomatoes, alfalfa, and corn. The fields are interrupted by olive plantations. All you have to do is hike along behind the dogs as they follow their nose.

"As a backdrop, there are the peaks of the Atlas Mountains, often blanketed in snow at the end of the year. . . ."

From time to time, you greet a *chibani* (an elderly person) wrapped up in his brown wool jellaba and who is philosophically tending his sheep, his chin resting on his cane and oblivious to your exploits. Contrary to what you sometimes hear, shooting quail is not always easy. The bird is lively, capricious, and unpredictable. True, sometimes it takes off in a straight line that often proves fatal to it. However, if there's any wind, it whirls like a bunch of dried grass, hesitates, twirls, and dodges the pattern of pellets.

The guide has spotted a quail; the hunter shoulders the gun and prepares to fire.

Hawks sweep down onto a rabbit with incredible speed. The rabbit gets away fairly often, thanks to some amazing maneuvers, but in this instance it was caught.

The Harris's hawk is very calm and likes to be petted. Its docile nature has made it a valued companion.

The rabbit has disappeared underground. The hawks are disappointed. Nothing short of a ferret will get it out of its hole.

Falconry: A Hunt for the Nobility

This is a magic realm where man puts on a different face, becomes a bird of prey himself, and flies up into the sky to track an elusive prey.

Hunting with falcons isn't like knocking over a wild rabbit, with a gun, and in your hiking boots. Falconry, like venery, is the arm of the nobility and horseback riders who appreciate hunting in the woods and flying in the fields. Like the horseman, the falcon is on a mission when it's after a partridge. In the early days, falconers practically considered the birds of prey to be human. They even distinguished between legitimate off-spring, born of parents of the same species, and illegitimate or mongrel offspring. The offspring of a saker falcon and a lanner was known as mongrel long before the term was applied to Anglo-French pack hounds. Falconry still claims a few hundred practitioners in Europe. The ritual has survived, whether in low flight or high flight, and the bonds that join people who hunt with falcons, eagles, and goshawks to their birds are almost mystical. It should be noted that training a bird is a tough undertaking that can occupy a man or a woman practically full-time. However, for some time, falconry has been adapting to modern times, if that's possible. Some falconers have found birds that are easier to train, and they even put on seminars for beginners. Even if this evolution causes the keepers of the flame to furrow their brow, it seems inevitable. The new raptors are Harris's hawks. They are close relatives to the falcon. In their favored biotope, in South America and the southern United States, they hunt in flocks, like wolves, and gang up on their prey. They are a handsome raptor about the size of a goshawk, tan colored with a white-banded black tail. The Harris's hawk has become quite popular because it's much more malleable than the goshawk.

"Hunting with falcons isn't like knocking over a wild rabbit. . . ."

You have to wear gloves to keep from getting punctured by the talons.

Wings outspread, the hawk has just struck a wild rabbit.

GRAB YOUR GUNS!

GRAB YOUR GUNS!

The notion of what constitutes game is subject to change. For centuries, anything that lived could be covered by this nonexclusive title: from the sparrow to the seal, the seagull to the peacock. The great classical still-life paintings are eloquent testimony to that.

"The list of species that are considered to be game animals has shrunk to almost nothing."

Along with partridge, hares, and ducks, you see orioles, penguins, goldfinches, and even poultry. The list of species that are considered to be game animals has shrunk to almost nothing. Nowadays, all species are protected except for the ones that are hunted. And every year, this list shrinks some more. In many parts of the world, you can no longer shoot swans, gulls, nor the little shoreline waders but with a few exceptions. People also distinguish between big and small game. The first category includes the large mammals; the second, the birds and small mammals. The value of the game depends on the country. The English consider rabbits and hares to be pests, but the French reserve a place of honor for

them. This value is also matched with a hunter's personal tastes. The hunters in the southwest of France have a real cult for wood pigeons, whereas the hunters in northern France and Europe in general don't pay them very much attention. The English, who are very selective, relegate it to the trash bin of nuisance creatures. Big-game hunters are very fond of records. They are filled with joy at the sight of a huge deer crowned with a massive set of antlers or an old wild boar approaching the line of fire. Ortolan hunters live, or rather once lived, for nothing more than to hunt this diminutive migratory bird. The woodcock, a revered bird, sends its aficionados into a trance, and the rabbit is capable of uniting thousands of followers in active hunting clubs. In France, where culinary pleasures count for a lot, wild game's gastronomic qualities are often included in its classification. The royal hare, the hunting rabbit, and a woodcock simply roasted have an appeal that no one can resist. That's one of the beauties of hunting.

From left to right:
Mixed bag of pheasants and red partridge.

Bag of woodcocks.

Thrushes.

Wood pigeons.

All these species belong to the great classics of small-game hunting.

Plucking the *painter's feather* is part of the ritual.

A beautiful harvested woodcock in the morning light. This is the reward for many hours of effort.

The Woodcock, Phantom of the Forest

I n France, Italy, and Quebec, the woodcock is the Holy Grail of small-game hunters. The bird bewitches and fascinates everyone who pursues it with dedication.

Why does the woodcock hold such a fascination for hunters? There are several reasons. One day it's there, and the next it has disappeared. Also, it has the most disconcerting habits. It changes its haunts according to the vagaries of the weather. You can never be sure of finding it again where you've once flushed it. Finally, the woodcock is the only game bird with a variable geometric flight: sometimes like a teal, sometimes like an owl, and at other times like a pheasant. The woodcock is capable of flying clumsily or, on the other hand, of taking off like a rocket. It's also a game bird that's very suitable for hunting with a bird dog. In 1758, the Swedish naturalist Carl von Linné classified the woodcock of the Eurasian strain under the name of *Scolopax rusticola*. Etymologically, the name comes from *skolops* (pointed) and from *rusticola* (living in the country). It's a name that emphasizes the bird's main feature: the pointed beak.

"The woodcock is capable of flying clumsily or, on the other hand, of taking off like a rocket."

This is a beak whose upper part is capable of opening at the end in order to capture the earthworms buried in the soil and that is equipped with tactile papillae that can also taste. Some birds, known as *brevirostrates*, have a short beak that varies in length between one inch and a little more than two inches (28 to 59 mm).

The eyes are large and dark. They are located on the top and toward the rear of the head, which appears somewhat flattened. These characteristics, plus the position of its eyes, give the woodcock a field of vision that encompasses almost the full 360 degrees. It can see nearly as well at night as during the day. The plumage is the woodcock's best protection since it blends in perfectly with the colors found in the underbrush. The coloration, which may vary significantly among individual birds, tends especially to browns dotted with shades and

With its velvety eye and its discreet conduct, the woodcock fascinates the hunter with its extensive bag of tricks and the intelligence it shows in outsmarting the dog. The quality of its flesh is also a valuable asset.

Excerpt from WOODCOCK STORIES
by Guy de Maupassant

"But there was in the house an old custom known as the 'woodcock story.' Just when this queen of game birds was passing through, the same ceremony resumed at every dinner. Since he loved this peerless bird, we all ate one in the evenings; but we took care to leave all the heads on the plates. Then the baron, officiating like a bishop, had a little fat brought to him on a plate, and then carefully anointed the precious heads by holding them by the end of the thin needle that serves them as a beak. A lighted candle was set near him, and everyone fell silent in anxiety and expectation. Then he would seize one of the heads thus prepared and impale it on a pin that he would then stick into a cork, holding everything in place with little crossed sticks like counterweights, and he would set this device delicately onto the neck of a bottle like a revolving display stand. All the guests would count together out loud, 'One, two, three.' And the baron would make this toy spin with a flick of his finger. The guest to whom the long beak pointed got all the heads, an exquisite delight that made all that person's neighbors eye him with envy. He would take them one by one and roast them over a candle flame. The fat would sizzle, the browned skin would smoke, and the person chosen by fate would crunch the tallowy skull as he held it by the beak and uttered expressions of delight."

mixtures of ash, reddish yellow, brown, and black on the bird's back. The breast exhibits some brownish transverse stripes. Dun-colored or totally albino woodcocks are quite rare; but partially albino ones are more common. So far, no melanotic (totally black) woodcocks have been found.

The weight varies between about nine and fourteen ounces (250 to 380 g), with a minimum of seven ounces and a maximum of about eighteen ounces (200 g and 500 g). The Eurasian distribution of the woodcock includes Europe out to the Atlantic islands (the Azores and the Canaries) and the British Isles, Asia as far as China, Mongolia, and Tibet. When considering the time period when the bird winters over, this area extends even as far as the coast of North Africa and Asia Minor. There are some species that live on Java, on Sumatra, and in the Celebes. The American variant is distributed throughout the entire North American continent.

"It likes woods with a preponderance of birch, acacia, chestnut. . . ."

The woodcock is a species that lives in the woods and ventures into open spaces only when it's looking for food or when it's fleeing danger. It likes woods with a preponderance of birch, acacia, chestnut, alders, larch, and beech, as well as fir and pine. It's better yet if the species are mixed and

Springer Spaniel retrieving. This dog has a soft mouth and doesn't crush the game; unfortunately, that's not always the case.

Study of woodcocks by Thorain (1975). The artist has captured the bird's positions perfectly.

"They plunge into the briars, hike for hours, and ignore rain and storm."

there has been no logging. Woodcocks are also frequently found among filberts, poplars, and oaks. They prefer mature forests between seven and twelve years old, not too dense, with a soft soil free of high grasses, where they can find food, peace, and a chance to hide or fly away easily.

Woodcock hunters tend to have a solitary nature. They have absolute confidence in their dogs—pointers, setters, and Brittany Spaniels—and they know their area like the back of their hand. They will spare no effort in going after their game. They plunge into the briars, hike for hours, and ignore rain and storm. Woodcock hunters tend to keep a running tally: one, five, fifteen, twenty, or even more on some exceptional days. They are also inclined to take off at least once a year for Ireland, which is like a natural conservatory for woodcock, and spend three or four days on the Emerald Isle. There you can hunt woodcock in three different biotopes: impenetrable firs, areas of underbrush known as the *bush*, and in the mountains, which are real backbreakers. A hunting guide known as a

A man and his dog in the forest in hopes of meeting a woodcock.

There's quite a bit of active discussion about the relative merits of the European woodcock and its American cousin. A lot of hunting camps have sprung up in Quebec, attracting numerous woodcock hunters who are all the more enthusiastic because they can bring their dogs and get a two-month jump in the season in France. In Quebec, the woodcock season opens around October 20. You hunt morning and afternoon in a radius of 50 to 330 feet (15 to 100 m) around camp. The terrain is flat, composed of woods and fields, and seems fairly familiar. You hunt at random as you explore every thicket. Aspens, alders, maples, and birch are the main species. Some sections are clear, and others are very dense—not too many briars, but tall grasses that hide felled tree trunks. You have to lift your feet high to avoid taking a spill. The American woodcock—smaller than the European variety—acts very much like its cousins. The same tricks, the same droppings, the same flushes like a rocket. However, it alights more quickly. The difficulty of the shot depends on the circumstances. Sometimes you hesitate to shoot so you don't turn it into confetti; at other times, the bird melts into the saplings twice as fast as the European woodcock. In any case, it's rare to shoot at more than about 20 yards (18 m). This is heaven for hunters who prefer the light-gauge guns.

"However, Ireland also holds some great days, sometimes with thirty birds in the game bag."

gillie goes with the hunters. He's the one who manages the bird dogs, which are Irish Setters, pointers, and Springer Spaniels. The hunting is hard, unpredictable, and full of surprises. You sink right up to midcalf in the marshland. You brave incredibly violent storms and squalls. You have to have a tenacious hold on life and be in good physical condition. However, Ireland also holds some great days, sometimes with thirty birds in the game bag. That's enough to make you forget the days when you come home empty-handed. Woodcocks are also choice morsels on the plate, and everyone comes up with recipes to bring out the best in them. In the old days, they were left hanging for two weeks, which amounted to eating decomposing meat. Nowadays, reasonable minds agree that a delay of a week in the cold weather is quite enough. A wonderful product of autumn, the woodcock deserves its reputation as the favorite quarry of the small-game hunter.

Breathtaking scenery above Courchevel, France.

Chamois and mountain goats are always on the lookout.

While perched in a
dip in the terrain,
this chamois hunter
searches the rubble.

Game from the Mountains

T he air is pure, the climb is very steep, the game is wild: the mountains don't attract the meek and are accessible only to the hardiest hunters.

Alpinus, a grand old master of the hunt, gives a perfect description of mountain hunting in his famous book *Alpine Hunting in Dauphiné.* That's a land where "the fare is meager, and the hunter becomes lean; where nothing abounds except fatigue; where the legs and the lungs have more work than the stomach; where every successful hunt attains the status of a conquest." Alpinus remarks further that this type of hunting, which is off-limits to the likes of bankers and lawyers, is pure hunting that rebuilds people and exalts their qualities, a hunt that banishes miasmas and ennobles the soul. The game you track on the mountain has the same characteristics: wild, independent, lean, and unpredictable. To those who persevere belong the rewards: the chamois is the first game that people go after on the high peaks. By stalking, of course. This is a solitary type of hunting. One man, pack on the back, shod in hiking

". . . the chamois is the first game that people go after on the high peaks."

Searching with binoculars or a spotting scope is the only way to locate an animal (here, above Embrun, France).

Alpine grouse also frequent the high mountains (here above Embrun, France).

boots, and binoculars hung around his neck, takes off following his nose into the vast expanses. This is the most beautiful of all ways to hunt!

The high mountains are dangerous. You mustn't venture into them without a guide. You also have to be in good physical shape, for you'll hike for long hours before returning to the valley. Don't forget to bring some food and a canteen of water, along with some warm clothing. The mountaineer hikes along silently and takes up a position on a lookout to glass the terrain with a pair of binoculars. When he spots the appropriate quarry, he tries to get as close as possible for a fatal shot. A scoped rifle is absolutely necessary for accurate long-distance shooting. Good choices of caliber include such stalwarts as the .270, 7 mm magnum, and .30–06. It's hard enough to get up to the altitude of the animals; climbing back down with 100 pounds (45 kg) of meat in your backpack is enough to bring a hunter to his knees.

The chamois hunter gets up early in the morning, usually around 4:30. He puts a hearty lunch into his backpack, along with 30 feet (9 m) of rope, a canteen filled with a mixture of wine and water, a flashlight, a knife, two clips, a bar of chocolate, some fruit, some sugar, and the game tag. The

Regardless of what French author Marcel Pagnol wrote, the rock partridge doesn't live anywhere near Marseilles, France. You have to get up into the summits of the Alps to find it. It's a really special game bird.

grab your guns!

Wood grouse hunting has a handful of passionate enthusiasts. They only hunt the males.

Excerpt from
LOOSE LEAVES FROM
MY HUNTING JOURNAL
by Wilhelm von Hohenzollern

"Once again I have to lower my rifle and wipe the scope lens with my handkerchief; these moments are really filled with anxiety. With one eye I continue to watch the chamois. Finally I'm ready; the rifle is poised, and with a light pressure on the trigger, the die is cast. The chamois jumps about four feet, then stops, backs up a few feet, makes a dash for the valley, now farther, now faster; finally it vanishes from view with another tremendous leap and a tumble, enveloped in a cloud of snow. 'Oh God, the horns! They'd better not be broken!' the hunter groans."

"You hunt with a pointer, and you always have one foot higher than the other. . . ."

hunting license determines precisely what kind of chamois can be taken, and the hunter has no room for error. The tag, which will be attached to one of the rear legs of the downed animal, corresponds to a particular age classification and sex. When equipped with all these accessories, the chamois hunter is transformed into a lookout man lurking in the shadows. Once he arrives in the zone he's been assigned, he must continually glass the mountain at regular intervals to spot the animals, which are equally alert. A mere rolling stone can cause a stampede!

After spotting a herd, the hunter has to examine each animal to see if there's one that matches his specific tag. If not, he puts his pack back on and resumes his long hike. One out of every three hunts will be successful. After eight hours of climbing around on the scree, the hunter returns to the valley totally exhausted.

In the foothills of the mountains, the forest carpeted with blueberries is the kingdom of the black grouse. Only the males are hunted. You hunt with a pointer, and you always have one foot higher than the other, balancing on a rock or a stump. Getting your feet tangled up in roots and taking a tumble commonly occurs. The black grouse takes off like a tornado and heads for the abyss. You'll get one or two chances, but rarely three. This is an athletic type of hunting, but it's almost a fitness stroll compared with hunting the white partridge and the grouse that live one

94

level higher in the middle of the breaks and the scree. That's when the mountaineer gets a chance to show his worth. Ten times a day, he gets to go back down a pitch he has just climbed and climb a pitch he has just gone down. The fickle grouse live in flocks that can range up to thirty birds. Their protective coloration is amazing, and a wounded bird is often a lost bird, unless you have a very good dog. The rock partridge live in smaller flocks. They are a magnificent prize that justifies the backaches and strains. This beautiful alpine bird looks like a red partridge but is distinguished by a uniform black bib around its neck (the red partridge's is merely spotted with black). This bird is very susceptible to predators, especially the golden eagle. Good alpine hunters know where the flocks are located and spread out over the terrain. Among the chamois, the partridge, and the grouse, which is the most captivating? It's hard to say, for everyone has a different preference. The chamois hunter doesn't switch to the rock partridge or the grouse, and the partridge hunter rarely switches to the chamois. Everyone has a specialty. What they have in common is a sense of amusement at the sight of a city slicker climbing up to them filled with nitric oxide and puffing like a bellows as he gets his feet tangled in the first blueberry bush he encounters. Alpinus was right: let's leave the mountains to the mountaineers.

"Among the chamois, the partridge, and the grouse, which is the most captivating?"

Chamois tracks.
Evidence of a highly
sought-after presence.

The retriever has
picked up the scent
of a wounded snow
partridge. Now to
retrieve it.

95

This hunter from the Sologne region in France intently examines his prey.

The Rabbit: A Game Animal That's Always Prized

Although decimated by myxomatosis in some parts of the world, the wild rabbit is still a cult animal that has generated some extraordinary efforts on behalf of its restoration.

Hundreds of rabbits shaking themselves at the edges of the woods, pieces of ground turned into Swiss cheese, devastated gardens—that's what most of the countryside was like at the start of the last century. The rabbit wasn't simply the hunter's favorite game that kept him from coming home empty-handed. It was also a destructive creature. That's why one man, Dr. Armand Delille, decided on June 2, 1952 to inject the myxomatosis virus into two rabbits on his property at Maillebois (Eure-et-Loire, France). He tied them into a sack and released them in the middle of a park. Nobody knew what he was up to, not even his farmworkers. Six weeks later, nearly all the rabbits at Maillebois had been exterminated.

"The rabbit wasn't simply the hunter's favorite game. . . ."

In an address presented on June 24, 1953 at the Academy of Agriculture, the experimenter justified his action by stating that French agriculture had suffered billions in losses due to rabbits. However, guess what: the epizootic wasn't confined to his property. One year later, nearly all of France was infected. Then Europe. With the support of the Saint Hubert Club of France, an organization was founded to combat "all types of epizootic that affect domestic and wild animals, especially myxomatosis." It pursued legal measures against Dr. Armand Delille and sought a symbolic restitution of one franc for damages and interest. It even gave an award to the doctor. It bears the inscription, "With gratitude from the forest and agriculture industries." In the final analysis, the hunters were the only ones who were adversely affected. Since that time, the rabbit populations have recovered somewhat, but waves of myxomytosis still ravage this game animal from time to time. People have tried everything to stem its spread. A vaccine, SG33, protects the

". . . the rodent guarantees a reliable source of hunting."

A pair of rabbits bagged with a 28-gauge. This type of gun is a perfect choice.

animal for six months. You also have to capture the rabbits in their warrens. They have also tried to introduce the Sylvilagus, or cottontail, a rabbit from Florida that has a resistance to the illness. The results have been inconclusive. Rabbit hunters in the south of France have gone so far as to establish a specialized laboratory, Bio-Space, and to create a program involving vaccinating fleas by filling them with vaccine that would immunize the rabbits down in their warrens. With some ups and downs, this program is running its course.

"Rabbits are a good game animal for young people and for oldsters. . . ."

With thousands of rabbits bagged each year, this animal is still in second place in the national tallies in France. That proves that despite the pressures of illness, the species is quite resistant. It is even abundant in some southern sections of France and on the islands of Oléron and Noirmoutier. It's true that this game is polygamous and remarkably prolific from February through August. It has from five to seven litters per year with four or five young per litter. Rabbits can adapt to most types of environment. You can find them just as readily on the plains as in the woods, in the hills, and at the edge of ditches, quarries, unplowed land, and scrub. Rabbits are a good game animal for young people and for oldsters who don't have the sharp eyesight they once had; the rodent guarantees a reliable source of hunting. The easiest way to hunt rabbits is still to follow your nose, with or without a dog. Hunting without a dog is possible, especially in the first days of the season, before the game becomes too skittish. In areas that have plenty of rabbits and where the vegetation isn't too thick, rabbits can flush from between your feet.

A rabbit from a vineyard. To the proprietor's joy, it won't eat any more of the young shoots.

These two rabbit hunters are past masters in hunting the hedgerows. They shot the game over point by the setter.

The Harris's hawk is a delight to hunters who like to use birds of prey on rabbits.

". . . the hunter's heart leaps when the little white flame bounds onto the grass."

However, having a dog along makes the outing more memorable. Cocker and Springer Spaniels are best suited to hunting close. You can also hunt with hounds like Bassets and Beagles.

In order to practice venery in France—taking rabbits with dogs while the hunters are unarmed—you have to have a *pack certificate* issued by the regional Agriculture and Forestry office. A good rabbit is capable of running for about an hour ahead of the pack. During the winter, some people hunt with ferrets. That involves introducing the animal into the opening of the burrow. A ferret is a small carnivore that belongs to the skunk family; it goes after the rabbit to grab it by the throat. When the rabbit bolts, the hunter is waiting at the mouth of the burrow.

The rabbit is a noble game animal. It's the basis of hunting in France. Even if it's considered on a local level to be a nuisance, the hunter's heart leaps when the little white flame bounds onto the grass. After a hard rain at night or a freeze in the morning, there's a good chance to find rabbits nestled along a wooded area, a hedge, a ditch, or a low stone wall. They like places that are exposed to the sun and sheltered from the wind. The

A ferret will bite a rabbit in the throat and may gorge on its blood. Afterward, it sometimes goes to sleep in the bottom of the warren. . . .

"The search for rabbits has to be slow and patient."

search for rabbits has to be slow and patient. The hunter will do well to keep an eye on the game trails, the most active of which are easy to spot. Shots are taken at short distance with a small-gauge, short-barreled gun loaded with small shot (8s or 9s).

Fifty acres (20 ha) with some artificial warrens are enough to hold a good rabbit population. Setting up spaces like this improves population density. They are set up in a well-drained area where flooding is not a threat. The work starts by cleaning out the vegetation with a brush-hog. Then some trenches are cut from top to bottom to facilitate runoff. Then you pile up logs and stumps to a height of about five feet (1.5 m). The tangle of wood creates a network that the rabbits can get around in. To make it waterproof, the whole thing is covered with a sheet of plastic and some more branches. Inside the warren, you can provide a few four-inch (10-cm) pipes leading to the exterior. They make capturing the rabbits possible in order to inoculate them and to fumigate the warren with insecticide if it becomes infested with carrier insects.

All dogs love this game, and sometimes they can't resist stepping out of line just a bit.

99

Mallards taking flight. And if weather conditions are good in the summer, dozens of young ducks will also take off.

Young mallards; the young ducks have brown plumage like the females. At the close of summer, the males will change their livery.

Shooting from a dam that cuts the swamp in two affords these hunters the chance to take some fine shots.

Yearling Ducks: Summer Around the Ponds

This hunter takes the precaution of protecting his eyes with shatter-resistant glasses.

ummer hunting, which is presently endangered, may one day enter the pantheon of vanished techniques.

Will people be able to continue hunting yearling ducks in some parts of the world? Nothing could be less certain. Ecology movements are fighting to end hunting in the summer. This type of hunting could thus be the next one to enter the pantheon of vanished techniques. The quarry here is year-old ducks. They are easily recognizable by their uniformly brown plumage. They look a lot like a mallard drake, but they are smaller. The drives are well organized, for the ducks are bred intensively. When the season opens, seeing several hundred young ducks on one body of water is common. Some of these birds were bred in hatcheries, purchased, and let loose.

In the Sologne region of France alone they raise four hundred and fifty to five hundred thousand young ducks. The yearlings are hunted in July and August around the ponds. The hunters hide their guns in the reeds near the water or on one of the small dams that frequently divide the ponds into two parts. The beaters drive the game toward the line of hunters by rowing or poling small boats since motors are not allowed. The first flight is the most fruitful one. After that, the birds return for some time and then, alerted by the gunshots, they vacate the premises until evening. Normally, the purely wild yearling ducks are the first to leave, followed by the hatchery ducks, which are heavier. Sometimes the hunters are surprised by the first flights. Hidden in the rushes, and with their faces stuck into the vegetation, they stand up too late and shoot behind the ducks. The results are mediocre early on, especially when you're out of practice from the off-season. The yearling ducks—at least the truly wild ones—defend themselves by flying over the line of hunters in a tight group. Sometimes one or two, or up to three, will fall, but rarely more. If they have been fed enough grain, they'll soon return and will fly around the pond. It's a big mistake to try to take them at the farthest range. That's the surest way to scare them off altogether.

"The hunters hide their guns in the reeds. . . ."

"Normally, the purely wild yearling ducks are the first to leave, followed by the hatchery ducks, which are heavier."

A Labrador is indispensable in retrieving downed birds.

The proliferation of fencing interferes with the movement of big-game animals. Still, sometimes it's necessary to protect the crops. Here a deer walks along an impenetrable barrier.

Seeing an animal once it's bedded down in the high grass is very hard.

Once the tag is attached to the animal, you can start the hike out.

Roe Deer, A Prolific Species

Nowadays you see deer everywhere. They are the proof that hunting and ecology can work together.

Once considered a somewhat rare game animal in some parts, the deer has become nearly as common as the rabbit. You see them everywhere: in the woods, of course, but also in fields, in swamps, and on fallow land. The deer population really exploded by the end of the twentieth century, and it has generated a real passion among the hunters who are only too happy for the windfall this presents.

The roe deer is the most elegant and the smallest of the European deer. Its coat varies from a truly stunning red to mousy gray. It has no obvious tail but a large white spot known as the mirror. The buck has antlers, but the doe has none. You can also distinguish between the sexes by the shape of the mirror: heart shaped in the does and elongated in the bucks.

"The roe deer sheds its antlers every year in November; they grow back by the end of March."

The roebuck is a homebody type of animal that could be content to spend its entire life in a few acres of woods. They are individualists who most often live alone and don't have much social life. The bucks mark their territory and admit no rivals. When it's frightened, a roe deer barks. The rut takes place from July 15 to August 15. The polygamous bucks try to conquer several does. The fawns are born ten months later, between May 15 and June 15. They vary in number from one to three. At the age of six months, the buttons, the first signs of antlers, appear; they fall off three months later. That's when the real antlers start to grow under the protection of a downy skin referred to as velvet. The roe deer sheds its antlers every year in November; they grow back by the end of March. It's normal to have six points (three per side). The antlers continue to grow larger for several years, and then they diminish with old age.

The classic type of hunt is a drive, the good old group drive with a line of hunters in position and a line of walking hunters. People aren't fussy, and they shoot any animal they flush.

Excerpt from TENDER BESTIARY
by Maurice Genevoix

"Anyone who has ever seen a roe deer jump a high fence at the edge of the woods to go browse in a field will always remember that wonderful bound, the outstretched neck, the knees drawn up in front until they almost touch the throat, the seemingly slow rise, so effortless, that carries the tawny body upward on an angle, the sudden folding of the rear legs as the animal clears the barbed wire, while at the front the legs are already deploying and reaching—changing from an oblique rise to a descent—to catch the animal's weight as it lands."

Above:
Roe deer tracks.

The number of antler points does not depend on the animal's age. A well-nourished deer will quickly develop a fine rack.

Two deer at a headlong run as seen by the illustrator Joseph Oberthur.

His Majesty the Deer: A Dream Trophy

S hooting a deer that sports a tremendous rack is one of the most cherished dreams of the big-game hunter.

"The hunter gets into action at dawn or in the twilight."

These are large but skittish animals. You don't see them during the day. However, at dawn or in the twilight, they come out of the forest making less noise than a field mouse. These are the trophy bucks, living monuments that mostly inhabit the eastern forests of Europe, even though some considerable animals are in France, too. The national record scored a little over 220 points. These magnificent antlers weigh more than twenty pounds (9 kg). The deer that wore them was found dead by a tracker in the Cote-d'Or Forest in the town of Saint-Jean-de-Boeuf. The gregarious deer lives in herds with very clearly defined pecking orders. They may be led by a buck or a doe. The rut takes place from mid-September to mid-October. The buck defends its territory and challenges its adversaries by emitting a hoarse call: it bugles. This is a good time to hunt it, as long as the season is open. Deer are hunted with drives as well as by still-hunting. However, the latter method of hunting is the most interesting one, for it allows the hunter to choose his animal. The hunter gets into action at dawn or in the twilight. You have to know where the big animals are bedded down during the day (sometimes with a brief period of activity around midday). They get up to go to their feeding areas only in the early hours of the morning and at sundown. The European trophy hunter uses accurate guns in an appropriate caliber—often single-shot rifles. The hunter dresses in camouflage, wears soft boots, and walks as carefully as the game. You have to spot the animal with your binoculars before it detects your presence. Once you've gotten that far, the identification process starts so the hunter can see if the deer is shootable or not. Big-game hunters are very demanding. They don't go to Bulgaria or Hungary for a week to shoot a mediocre animal, and they would prefer to return home to wait for their dream to materialize into a larger animal.

Scottish stag on the shore of a lake. Raising these animals gives the farmer a good source of pocket money.

Above: This wonderful animal has always inspired artists. Here, an oil painting from the middle of the twentieth century.

Left: Herd of young deer. The antlers drop off from February to May, only to grow back covered with a delicate coating known as *velvet*.

"Rocket" Partridge: Myth or Reality?

Destruction of countryside by mechanized agriculture has been a hard blow to all partridge.

The gray partridge needs diversity in its habitat.

All postwar hunting writers talk of a little migratory partridge, the rocket, which descended onto the fields during the migrations. In spite of contemporary witnesses, scientists remain skeptical.

It was a real windfall, manna that fell from the sky. The hunters of yesteryear would rejoice when the migratory partridge, which they called rockets, arrived on the plains. These birds would stay for a day or two and then leave again. These birds were, according to witnesses, like gray partridge yet different: a slightly longer beak, smaller in size, and with yellow legs. In the 1920s, nobody questioned the existence of the rockets. A hunting author named Alfred Delecour devoted a whole chapter in his book *Wild Game of France* to this game bird and gave ample support to the thesis of the migratory partridge.

The most extraordinary observation concerns the invasion of a garden right in the center of the town of Saint-Quentin in northern France. "At the end of the month of October 1928, around three o'clock in the afternoon, my father was in his garden located at 15 d'Aumale Street, which is right in the center of town, at a distance of at least 1,500 to 1,800 yards/meters from the fields, when he heard the noise of wings in the large trees and he saw a flock of twelve to fifteen partridge arriving at high speed and looking for a place to roost. One of them in fact perched on the wall; some of them came down on a lawn, others perched on the low branches of the chestnut trees. My father went to get his gun, returned to his garden, and fired at the partridge that had landed on the wall. It was small and had all the characteristics of the rocket partridge." Greatly enthused by this topic, Alfred Delecour struck up a relationship with an inspector of the Woods and Waters Department named Saby, who likewise was interested in the phenomenon and who had edited a detailed monograph on the subject. Here are some excerpts from it: "... Having sought to account for the large flights of rockets in the Yonne Department, we were very surprised to learn that this phantom bird had always come to nest in our region; just like the quail, they would

"In the 1920s, no one questioned the existence of the rockets."

Snow condemns the partridge to famine.

The rocket partridge as seen by Joseph Oberthur. More slender than a normal gray?

arrive in April and nest in May, and the young would hatch in June, leaving in October or November for their unknown winter range. . . ." He adds, "It's quite difficult to admit that a bird the size of the rocket can always nest, or at least that it has long nested, sixty miles [100 km] from the capital of France without this fact being known to all the ornithologists, and that hundreds of hunters kill them by the thousands every year without doubting that they have downed a partridge that's different from the ordinary gray partridge. But that is evidently the case, however extraordinary it may seem."

As another witness for the defense, Oberthur also pleads in favor of this strange partridge: "On April 6, 1953, I saw a curious flight of partridge in Cancale that came from the east and headed toward the southwest, a very abnormal direction for the season. I counted more than a hundred birds. They came from the Contentin coast, so they had flown over the ocean for at least twelve miles [19 km], and they flew over my garden." Some scientists approach this subject soberly. From a morphological point of view, for example, the partridge has the capacity to travel long distances. "The water rail is a poor flier, but it can still migrate; so why not the partridge?" asks the ornithologist Nicolau-Guillaumet. This researcher at the Center for Research on Bird Populations, who has examined thousands of migratory birds, has never found a rocket. Just the same, he does not discount the possibility that a migratory partridge exists. The mystery remains intact.

"Just the same, he does not discount the possibility that a migratory partridge exists."

Snow geese populations are constantly increasing in North America.

A snowstorm sweeps across the frozen expanses. The hunting has been good.

It's usual to shoot geese on the wing. This is a posed snapshot.

One Snow Goose Is Worth Two Canadas!

Snow goose populations are exploding in North America. The daily bag limit is twenty per hunter.

What wonderful game birds! Not many birds can quicken the pulse of waterfowl devotees the way these birds can. Of course, the Canada geese are nothing to sneeze at. However, the snow geese are something else entirely. You might say that one snow goose is worth two Canadas. You hunt snow geese by setting out decoys on frozen fields. The guides are robust and friendly boys dressed in camouflage suits and a bandolier of a half-dozen calls. Each one produces a different sound. There is a long-distance call to turn a flock in flight, a close-range call to hold their attention, a confidence call to bring them in, and a call that's used to bring them back if they're moving away. The blind is a simple depression dug into the ground. Straw is placed around to help the hunter blend into the countryside. The guides join in the action like concert musicians playing a duet. While one blows on a long-distance call, the other i whispers into a confidence call to reproduce the sound the geese make when they are eating under the watchful eye of their lookouts. You listen to the recital in stereo. The virtuosity of these guides is remarkable. I have seen them climb out of the blind, and like the Pied Piper of Hamlin who charmed the rats, walk in the open toward the geese without startling them to flight!

Snow geese populations (up to seven hundred thousand individuals) are continually increasing in Quebec, and that makes the farmers break out in a cold sweat. Unlike the large Canada geese, which are content to eat sprouts, the snows eat the roots, which is a different kind of aggravation. The Canadians don't have any particular qualms about wildlife. If a population goes down, they restrict the bag limits; if it increases, they up them. That's the situation with the snow geese, whose daily bag limit is set at . . . twenty! This is a windfall for foreign hunters.

"The guides join in the action like concert musicians playing a duet."

The local guides can use their calls not only to pull the birds in but even to walk up to them in the open!

Searching for a Black Diamond

This is a great trophy, but given the declining populations, it's increasingly difficult to bag one of these birds. An astounding takeoff, a dizzying nosedive into the abyss, a heavy fall onto the carpet of blueberries: taking a capercaillie, or European wood grouse, is enough to leave even the most jaded hunter speechless.

The capercaillie, or wood grouse, which is as large as a turkey, is becoming increasingly rare despite protective measures that have been instituted in the Pyrenees. It has disappeared from Vercors, Chartreuse, Tarentaise, Beaufortin (in 1975), and Chablais (1992). In the French Alps, only a dozen specimens are left in the upper Giffre valley in Haute-Savoie. There are still about three hundred in the Vosges, four hundred in the Juras (compared with eight hundred in 1960). . . . Only the nucleus in the Pyrenees seems to be stable, with a little less than five thousand individuals, which are part of a particular subspecies. This is an imposing bird that sends delightful shivers up the spine of the Alpine hunter. In early autumn, you can hunt the males. Only for a few days. In the eastern countries, the wood grouse is hunted regularly by calling them when they are strutting. The technique involves approaching the bird as it calls, for during this brief instant, it loses all suspicion. Hunting starts just after winter. During the cold season, the bird spends most of its time on the branch of a spruce or a fir, peeling the bark and eating the needles, moving as little as possible to avoid wasting energy. As soon as the vegetation season reawakens, the males get together early in the morning on their parade grounds. At this time, certain individuals behave strangely. These crazy cocks are not common, but their numbers seem to be on the increase. According to a study conducted by the National Hunting Office, 134 cases of aberrant behavior were recorded in France, Switzerland, and Italy. Certain ones among these cocks have been observed in the company of domestic hens but never in the presence of other males. The hens start to lay around the end of April. They may lay

"This is an imposing bird that sends delightful shivers up the spine of the Alpine hunter."

During the mating season, the male wood grouse fans out his tail to intimidate possible competitors.

Typical underbrush in the Cévennes preserve. The big bird needs evergreens, and not too many pine martens, in order to thrive.

110

The Cévennes forest near Florac in France's central mountain range. For several years, people have been trying to reintroduce the capercaillie, or wood grouse.

from ten to sixteen eggs. However, the hatches are less and less successful, for the wood grouse are continually disturbed. There are some ongoing efforts to reintroduce them, particularly in the Cévennes preserve. However, the experiment is so far not very convincing even though there is now a nucleus of reproducers.

The measures taken to encourage development of the species will consist of limiting the use of the abundant forest trails only to professionals in order to preserve the peace that the wood grouse need. It's also necessary to conserve the Scotch pines, which the birds seek out in the winter, and to outlaw grazing in the underbrush to encourage population regeneration. Also, predators clearly play a very important role in the stagnation of the species. That's why the Scottish, for example, have systematically destroyed the predators in the areas that the cocks inhabit. And the fox populations in the British Isles have been seriously reduced. Unfortunately, though, the fox is not the only predator of the wood grouse. Stone martens, ermine, boars, and jays can destroy the eggs and even kill the youngest birds. Also, the martens have no hesitation, despite their small size, in attacking the adults. Then there's the main enemy of the great birds: man, with his propensity to wreck the habitat to set up his own play areas.

"The hens start to lay around the end of April. They may lay from ten to sixteen eggs."

Aggressive posture of a male defending his territory.

is large wood grouse is taking a dust bath. This is a preference it shares with gallinaceous birds such as chickens and partridges.

The Wolf: From Public Enemy to Noble Savage

Wolves, which are staging a comeback nowadays, were considered a scourge until the start of the nineteenth century. They were the object of some infernal hunts that lasted for days at a time.

At the present, about twenty wolves imported from Italy are living in southern France. They get their food in part from sheep in the summer and from wild ungulates in the winter. Biologists are unanimous in their opinion that wolves do not attack humans. However, ancient chronicles are filled with tales that indicate the contrary. Let's have a look at history. Wolf or werewolf? A creature of God or a demon escaped from hell? The ancestral terror that the wolf generated seems to be the complex result of real misdeeds and religious superstitions. Throughout the Middle Ages, people were persuaded that the devil was able to transform people into wolves. Everyone had his own brand of proof. Here there was a girl who was abducted and raped by a man covered with hair; there, a little boy disemboweled by a creature of the same appearance; farther away, an ecclesiastic who "dissolved" the hateful creature in a shower of holy water.

"Wolf or werewolf? A creature of God or a demon escaped from hell?"

And that wasn't just a peasant belief reserved for simple people. In all social classes, including the most erudite, the fear of the werewolf existed. On January 18, 1574, the parliament at Dole, in eastern France, condemned a certain Gilles Garnier to death by being burned alive for "four murders committed on girls and boys, whose flesh he devoured while he was in the shape of a wolf," according to his own confession. At the beginning of the seventeenth century, many people still believed that excommunicated people and those who had not taken the sacrament at Easter could be transformed into werewolves.

The French King Charlemagne created a corps of wolf hunters. In a capitulary of 813, he ordered his counts to designate in their district two officers whose duties would consist of hunting wolves. He also wanted to know how many had been killed and asked to see their skins. These

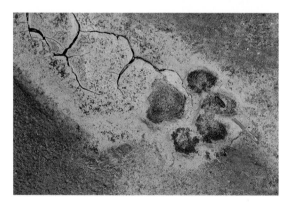

Wolf tracks.

Wolves shot near Poitiers, France, at the end of the nineteenth century. Widespread poisoning precipitated the disappearance of this animal, which was then regarded as a curse.

Excerpt from THE GENTLEMEN HUNTERS
by the Marquis de Foudras

"The damned wolf, as if it understood the vow that we had made to send no more lead after it, didn't even take the trouble to be careful, didn't deign to stick its nose up into the air to see where the wind was coming from.
From time to time, we increased our pace to cut the wolf off and force it with our fanfares to retrace its steps, but what do you bet the rascal didn't pass right under the bell of our hunting horns with unspeakable impudence and break through as easily as if we hadn't even been there to hinder its movements. . . . Once a fairly long bridge lay in its path. The bridge was blocked by four or five farm carts surrounded by a huge flock of sheep walking in tight formation. The cart drivers had cause for concern, and the sheep were in a worrisome position; but what do you think that wolf did? It was neither cowardly nor careless, and it crossed the bridge with all the calm of a hero and the moderation of a philosopher.
I never saw anything so bizarre in all my life."

officers had quartering rights, and they sometimes abused them by robbing the peasants. That's why in 1395, King Charles VI required them thenceforth to sleep in country inns and to pay for everything they took or else be liable to the justice of the realm.

Did wolves really eat men, women, and children? There is abundant evidence for that. However, they were also reputed to dig up the dead. Here's the testimony of a middle-class man: "In 1421 or 1422, the wolves were so hungry that they would use their paws to dig up the bodies of people who were buried in the villages and the fields; for wherever you went, you would find dead people in the fields and in the cities, from the great poverty that afflicted them because of the damned war that kept increasing daily, from bad to worse. . . ." In the course of the year 1423, wolves entered Paris every night, and sometimes three or four were caught in a single night. The next day, the people who had caught them would parade through the city carrying the carcasses suspended from a pole, and "they were given money aplenty." In 1428, famine again ravaged Paris, and wolves roamed in the city, devouring children. The Office of Public Accounts would pay twenty sols to anyone who brought

"In 1428, famine again ravaged Paris, and wolves roamed in the city, devouring children."

Here the animal seems to be risking a good deal more than the man. . . .

Woodcut by Jost Amman dating from 1592.

". . . the peasants practiced self-defense largely with pitchforks, pikes, pits, and trained dogs."

in the head of a wolf. Wolves were hunted with hounds, including a few added greyhounds for speed, for wolves have the endurance to keep it up for hours. It was hard to get good wolf dogs! The animal doesn't give up easily, and it would often kill the dogs, which hardly dared to get close to it, or they would run back with their tail between their legs once they caught its scent. So they had to be hardened to the task. For that purpose, when they were young, they were made to devour young wolves that were caught in a trap. In spite of these precautions, catching old wolves was difficult. Mostly young ones were caught. That's why wolves were rarely hunted over a pack of hounds. People preferred traps, snares, poisoned bait, pits, and noisy drives under the direction of the officers of the wolf hunters. However, the traps worked against them, for as one chronicler of the era noted, they were "fatal to travelers who were not warned of their presence. . . ."

If wolves enjoy some esteem today, that wasn't the case in those days, when everyone hated the "evil beast." The struggle against wolves gradually became organized. In the country, the peasants practiced self-defense largely with pitchforks, pikes, pits, and trained dogs. The officers from the wolf-hunting unit hunted with hounds and used large-scale drives. When they organized wolf drives, the entire population had to take part, under "penalty of a ten-pound fine for the shirkers."

The Royal Wolf Hunters expanded under Louis XIV because the heir apparent was bored, and that became his favorite unit. He would often leave Versailles before daylight to attack a wolf in the woods of Saint-Germain, Rambouillet, or Marly and return just in time for the king's mass. Eighty horses champed at the bit in the royal stables, and that was hardly enough. For horses used for hunting wolves were simply a means of transportation. The idea was to pursue the animal until the horse tired, to jump on a fresh mount, and to resume the chase.

Kings passed, and wolves remained, and the supply seemed inexhaustible. Louis XVI distinguished himself from his predecessors by creating a chaplain's post in the wolf-hunting unit. At that time, the royal wolf-hunting unit killed three hundred wolves a year. During the night of August 4, 1789, all the privileges of the nobility were abolished, including hunting. On August 11, a decree established the right of all property owners to destroy any kind of game on their lands during an "open season" and to kill harmful animals, including wolves, at all times. The Emperor Napoleon placed wolf hunting under the direction of a master huntsman. The wolf was still a species that deserved to be eradicated, as indicated by a report of the French Agricultural Society

"At that time, the royal wolf-hunting unit killed three hundred wolves a year."

Engraving by
Joan Galle (ca.
1600–1676),
based on
Stradamus.

from around 1870: "Presently there is one species too many among our wildlife: wolves, which should have disappeared entirely from our territory more than a century ago." Things then started to go hard on the species. In 1884, 1,034 wolves were killed, including twenty-two pregnant females; in 1892, 307, including six pregnant females; and in 1896, 171, including one pregnant female. The figures tell the story. . . . However, they match the stated purpose: the eradication of the species. That was finally accomplished shortly before the Second World War . . . until the wolves reappeared at the end of the twentieth century in the foothills of the Alps.

Left: Fantasy or reality? The beast of Gévaudan was pictured many times, and in very formidable proportions in this woodcut.

Below: In another representation of the beast, the girl is saved from a horrible death at the last possible moment.

The Beast of Gévaudan: A Mystery Never Resolved

All hunters at the end of the eighteenth century hoped to kill the beast of Gévaudan. In 1767, Jean Chastel killed an enormous female wolf with "a blessed bullet," and the depredations ceased. However, there are still a lot of gray areas in this strange affair.

What creature was it that for three years, from 1764 to 1767, killed, mutilated, or devoured a hundred people in the Ardeche, the Upper Loire, and Cantal regions of France? Even today the mystery is intact. Even if Jean Chastel did kill an enormous wolf in 1767, thereby ending the depredations, many people today think that more than one animal was responsible. There probably was one or more "serial killers," perhaps accompanied by domesticated animals that lent their aid. It all started in the summer of 1764. Sinister reports arrived from Langogne, on the upper Allier River. A woman had been attacked by a wild animal while she was tending her flocks. She returned to the village injured and with her apron ripped off and her clothing in shreds. She described a strange wolf with a very elongated head and a tremendous mouth. The wolf was reddish with a thick and fluffy tail and a black stripe on its back. At the beginning of July, a girl from Habats in the Vivarais region was devoured. From that point on the horror grew; another girl, and then a young boy were killed in the same circumstances. A whole series of identical events followed. The beast came and went, striking at different places, often very distant from one another. It was as fast as the wind, unpredictable, and impossible to catch in spite of drives conducted by the lords of the region. Was it the devil? The priests thought so, so they assembled their flock and made them pray. The rumor spread that dragons were intervening and killing dozens of wolves, but the beast continued to strike. *The Great Gazette of France*, the official mouthpiece of the king and the kingdom, got hold of the affair. The craziest theories began circulating. There was talk of a lycaon, or wild dog, that supposedly had been imported from Africa. A bounty of ten thousand pounds was

"Sinister reports arrived from Langogne, on the upper Allier River. A woman had been attacked by a wild animal. . . ."

Representation of the beast of Gévaudan; eighteenth-century engraving.

The beast of Gévaudan: often wounded but never killed. . . .

The beast of Gévaudan was reputed to have killed a hundred people between 1764 and 1767.

"But it kept coming back, apparently unharmed."

offered to anyone who succeeded in killing it. The local authorities increased the huge drives in which lots and lots of wolves were killed—but not the beast, which kept up its regular slaughter. The strange thing is that numerous victims survived the attacks, and those who weren't speechless with fright were able to describe the animal. According to some of them, it was a wolf; according to others, it was a wild dog or maybe the African lycaon that had been mentioned so often but was never seen. One thing was sure: it had a square head, a very broad jaw, and a stripe on the back. Was it a hyena? A mastiff? The beast was hit by a number of bullets, and it was stabbed repeatedly with pikes and pitchforks. But it kept coming back, apparently unharmed. That was pretty troubling! Now the dead were counted by the hundreds. Then François Antoine, the king's gun bearer, was brought to the scene. . . . He drew a blank, just like the others. The mystery was growing more intense when suspicion was directed toward Antoine Chastel, a strange fellow, a dirty, bearded woodsman who was said to have visited menageries in Algeria. Suppose the beast had a master? The man was imprisoned with his brother and his father, just for good measure. However, after a respite, the sinister events started anew. In the course of numerous drives, François Antoine managed to kill a huge wolf that he thought was the right one. It weighed 130 pounds (59 kg) and was five feet, seven-and-a-half inches (1.7 m) long. Witnesses came to view the corpse and recognized it. Relief. The Chastels were released. However, the peace didn't last long, and three months later, the depredations started again. Some attacks bore all evidence of being perpetrated by a human, like the one against a girl who was slashed, partly devoured, and yet dressed after death so that when she was found she "appeared to be asleep." In high places, people no longer spoke about a beast, since officially it had been killed, but of "carnivorous wolves." Consternation reigned in the area. No one knew how to put an end to the curse. On June 19, 1767, one more drive brought together three hundred hunters. Jean Chastel, Antoine's father, took part in it. According to Jacques Denis, a contemporary witness, he read the litanies of the Virgin when the beast appeared before him. He took "the time to finish them," we are told, shouldered his piece, and "knocked the beast of Gévaudan dead with a blessed bullet." Ever since, "no grass has grown at that spot." It was a large, reddish, male wolf, very different from normal wolves, that weighed 109 pounds (50 kg). The bone from a girl was found inside it. A local barber embalmed the remains and sent them to Paris. It was a long trip, and the wolf didn't survive. When it arrived at the capital, it was fully decomposed. It was quickly buried. Was that really the culprit? Or did the murderer and his wild animal decide to end the misdeeds? Whatever the case, the attacks ceased, and that was the end of the curse of the beast of Gévaudan.

". . . he read the litanies of the Virgin when the beast appeared before him."

Presentation of the beast of Gévaudan to King Louis XV and the royal family. The "beast" had been embalmed and mounted on a plank. Was it the right animal? No one knows for sure. . . .

PHOTO CREDITS

All photos are by Eric Joly, except:

Fanny Bruno: 12–13, 14 (top left and bottom), 15 (top right, center, and bottom).**Corbis Sygma:** Bettmann (cover). **Côtés Vues:** L. Maisant 6–7; A. Lorgnier 10 (top right and center). **D. R.:** 42–43. **Manufrance:** 22–23. **Périnet:** 32–35. **Roger-Viollet:** 10 (lower right), 11, 16 (top right, center, and lower left), 17 (top, center, and lower right), 18–19, 20 (right), 21, 99 (bottom), 113, 114–115, 116–119. **Sunset:** J. J. Cournut 102 (top); FLPA 84–85, 107 (top), 111 (center right); G. Lacz 8 (left), 64 (bottom), 65 (lower right), 74 (lower left); Levin 112 (center and bottom); R. Maier 74 (top right), 106 (bottom), 111 (bottom); C. Simon 92 (top right); F. Stock 46–47; Weiss 87 (right), 95 (top right), 102 (lower left), 103 (bottom).

LEGENDS FOR COVER PHOTOS

Cover: Hunting scene from Tunkhannock, Pennsylvania;
pages 6–7, Hunting Museum at Montpoupon Château;
pages 18–19: hunting lions in Africa by Frederick Courtenay Selous;
pages 46–47: duck hunting in Canada;
pages 84–85: red deer, *Cervus elaphus.*

LITERARY EXCERPTS

Hunting Illustrated journal, 1867
Jean Castaing, *The Meaning of Hunting,* La Toison d'or, 1954
Guy de Maupassant, *Stories and News* (vol. I), la Pléiade, 1974
Wilhelm von Hohenzollern, *Loose Leaves from my Hunting Journal,* Fontemoing, 1913
Maurice Genevoix, *Tender Bestiary,* Plon, 1969
Marquis de Foudras, *The Gentlemen Hunters,* Pygmalion/Gérard Watelet, 1987

Designed and produced under copyright for Solar Editions
Graphic design: Ute-Charlotte Hettler
Layout: Odile Delaporte
Cover: Claire Brenier
Editorial coordination: Isabelle Raimond
Translated from the French by Eric A. Bye, M.A.